秋山孝のMacイラスト講座 コンピュータで感性を極める超初級技法

Takashi Akiyama **Getting Started as a Mac Illustrator**

まえがき

イラストレーターのぼくが、なぜ今さらコンピュータを使ってイラストレーションを描かなければならないのか。それを考えるとひとつのことに突き当たります。それは、現代の技術を応用した「視覚表現における美の可能性」を求めていることにほかなりません。

新しいことを試みることを一般的に「冒険」と呼んだりします。ぼくは、少年の頃から「冒険」というキーワードを耳にすると、胸がキュンとなってしまう。そこには、かつて読んだ冒険小説や、冒険マンガのストーリーが頭に浮かびます。必ずやって来る嵐や危険を乗り越えて、ひとつひとつ解決する勇気に感動します。さらにそこには、胸踊る夢やパラダイスが待っています。

いままで、一度も経験しなかった「視覚表現」に出会って、その表現の展開や広がりを思うと、希望に胸がふくらみ、冒険をしたくなる思いにかられます。これは、少年が前向きに自分の未来に向かって、夢想する喜びに近い。たしかに、乗り越えなければならない関門はあるが、夢と希望の力を借りてバージョンアップしたり、アップグレードしたいものです。

この「Macイラスト講座」は、Macのマニュアル（使用説明書）ではなく、コンピュータで感性を極める超初級技法であって、この本を読んでMacが作動しないとか、ソフトが開かないという苦情を持ち込まれても、この本では対応できません。目的が違うからです。まずは、Macの基本的操作を理解した人を前提としています。そうしないと感性についての話まで進まないからです。いつまでもデジタル操作とソフトの使い方だけになってしまいます。

この本をいちばん理解して、活用し、座右の書にできる対象は、美術に興味があり、いままでの表現様式から一歩前に進みたい前向きな姿勢を持った人。それらの人たちのための技法書として、さらに自分の表現を生み出すための踏み台や掛け橋になることを願っています。

しかし、シンプルな表現技法からもそれなりに面白くて、楽しい表現の展開があるということを証明したい。これをぼくは、ステコン技法（ステンドグラス・コンピュータ技法 解説 p.14）と呼んでいます。そこには、コンピュータという道具を超えたもうひとつの表現世界があります。すぐに思い通りの作品が描けないからといって、決して、単純な技法だからと言ったり、ソフトの限界のせいにしてはなりません。視覚表現は本人自身の感性や心の問題に深く根ざしています。

それらを踏まえて、この本を土台に未知の表現への冒険に旅立ってほしい。

“ Welcome to Macintosh World for Illustrators. ”

秋山孝
目白の仕事場にて

Introduction

When I ask myself why, as an illustrator, I must now use a computer to do my illustrations, I ultimately hit upon this answer: I want to discover the aesthetic possibilities of this modern form of visual expression. It is that simple.

Trying new things is generally referred to as "adventuring." Since my youth, the word "adventure" has always been one of my keywords. Each time I heard it, my heart would begin to race as I remembered adventure comics and tales I had read. The process of bravely overcoming obstacles, one by one, and the dreams of paradises which lay beyond, has never failed to intrigue me.

When for the first time I was confronted with "visual expression," and thought about the process of developing and expanding a visual creation, I felt my heart filling with hope, and the desire once again to adventure. This feeling was not unlike a youth's ecstatic hopes for the future. Of course there were barriers to success, but by the strength of these hopes and dreams I intended to upgrade, to version-up.

This "Getting Started as a Mac Illustrator" is not a Macintosh manual, but an ultra-beginner's guide to discovering your feelings on a computer. If you buy this book and can't already work your Mac, or open a software application, don't expect to find the answers here. That's not what this book is about. I assume you have a working knowledge of the Macintosh, lest the discussions of digital operations and software go on forever.

This book is most perfectly suited to those interested in art, and to those who wish to take a step beyond their current modes of visual creation. It is my hope that this book will provide these people with methods, or at least a springboard, by which to achieve their goals.

I also want to prove that there is an easy, but nevertheless interesting, way to create visual works. I call this method "stacom" (from stained glass and computer, see p.14) In this method, one transcends the computer, entering a new realm of visual expression. It cannot be criticized as being simplistic, or limited by software. The only limiting factor is the user's own heart and feeling.

By using this book you can begin your own adventure into an unexplored world of visual expression.

ステコン技法で制作したイラストレーション・目白1991
An illustration using the Stacom method. Mejiro,1991

“ Welcome to Macintosh World for Illustrators. ”

Takashi Akiyama
at Mejiro Office

もくじ

Contents

Getting Started as a Mac Illustrator

Copyright ©1994 by Graphic-sha Publishing Co., Ltd.
1-9-12 Kudan-kita, Chiyoda-ku, Tokyo 102, Japan

ISBN4-7661-0769-1

Printed in Japan
First Printing, 1994

Chapter

W● なぜ、「Macイラスト講座」を出版しようと思ったの?
Why did I think of publishing "Getting Started as a Mac Illustrator"?

ぼくは美術大学で教えているのだけれど、若い美術学生のためにも、入門書あるいは技法書が必要です。そして新しい表現様式を理解するときには、それに対しての方法論が必要になってくるからです。それで、Macのイラストレーションの入門書を作ろうと思いました。若い美術学生が、何かを表現するときに通過点として、理解し未来に向っていくときの掛け橋になるように、この本を出版したいと思いました。

*新しい表現様式

*Macのイラストレーションの入門書

*new techniques of illustration

*beginner's guide to illustrating on the Mac

I am currently teaching at an art college, but I felt that a beginning guide or technique book was needed for young art students. In order to understand the new techniques of illustration a methodology of some kind was required. That is how I hit upon the idea of a beginner's guide to illustrating on the Mac. I wanted this book to be a bridge to awareness of the future possibilities for young artists.

マッキントッシュルーム・ニューヨーク 1989
Macintosh Room. New York, 1989

W● 秋山孝のMacの超初級技法ってなに?
What is Akiyama Takashi's Ultra-Basic Methodology?

このMacの超初級技法を作ろうと思ったきっかけは、Macの入門書がまだ完成されていないように思えたからです。というのは、たとえば水彩技法、アクリル技法、油絵技法、日本画技法、テンペラ技法など、いろいろな絵画の技法において、入門書では感性や表現することの喜びをうまく伝えています。

*入門書

コンピュータの本は、見ただけで使うのがいやになりそうな、難しくて無味乾燥な感じがします。そういうのに慣れていない人は対応ができません。そこで、できるだけ簡単で、誰でもが入りやすい入口を作ってみたらいいと考えました。

まず、本は楽しくなくてはなりません。Macのマニュアルは、操作中心で動かすことやハードについての本が多い。だからそういったものではなくて、油絵や水彩やコンテなどで描くことの楽しさと同じような入口を、解りやすく作ってみたいと思いました。というのは、ぼく自身がコンピュータから入ったのではなく、表現すること、絵を描くことの興味からMacというデジタルの表現様式へと入ってきたからです。

*デジタルの表現様式

そしてMacの超初級技法を、水彩技法、アクリル技法、油絵技法、日本画技法、テンペラ技法のような絵画技法の中に、デジタルで表現ができるものとして位置づけてみたい。

*beginner's guides

I developed the ultra-basic methodology while waiting for the first Mac beginner's guides to appear. The idea is for the guide to convey the joy of all the techniques of expression - watercolor, acrylic, oil, Japanese ink, tempera, etc. - presented in its chapters.

Computer books are painful to the eye. They look hard to use, not to say dull. People who aren't accustomed to using them can't make sense of the explanations. My idea was to create a book as easy-to-use as possible, one anyone could take up as a beginning guide.

*digital expression tool called the Mac

First of all, the book had to be fun. Most books on the Mac center on how to work the system or hardware. So I wanted to begin with the enjoyment of using oils, watercolors, contes, and other mediums, in other words to make pleasure the point of departure - just as I myself started using the digital expression tool called the Mac not from a need to learn about the computer, but from an interest in painting and visual expression.

Thus the idea of an ultra-basic Mac methodology is to establish the computer as a digital tool to be tried within the fields of watercolor, acrylic, oil, Japanese ink, tempera, etc.

●コンピュータで感性を極めることができるって、ほんと？
Is it true you can express feeling on the computer?

*感性

ぼくは、感性とは「感じること、物事を見て心が動くこと」と考えています。

心が動いてその喜びや衝撃、感動をいままで絵かきレベルでは、鉛筆や油絵の具で描いたりするけれど、コンピュータは、操作中心でどうしても表現の感性がいきづまりそうです。でも、ある種の技法を用いれば、キーボードを打ちながらマウスを動かしながらでも、モニターやプリントアウトしたものを通して、自分の持っている喜びや感動を極めることができると思います。

『にじみ』ステコン技法 1992
"Ooze" Stacom method, 1992

*feeling

I think of feeling as "sensing, and the movement of the heart brought about by the confrontation with an object."

The joy and power of the heart in motion is readily evident in drawings and paintings, but when one turns to the computer it seems that the expression of feeling is often blocked. But I believe that by hitting the keyboard, moving the mouse, viewing the monitor and printing out works, one can experience the joy and emotion of artistic expression.

I ● Macが才能を引き出してくれるって、ほんと？
s it true that a Mac will bring out your talent?

Macの中に入っているソフトは自立しています。Macをいじることによって、ソフトを読み取ったり、利用したりすることがMacの在り方です。Macのソフトの限界は超えられないけれど、もともとできているものを応用し、組み合わせたり、どれを引き出すかはいろいろ考えられます。Macで表現しようとすることによって、その人なりのセンシビリティから、限られた条件の中で個人の才能と可能性は十分引き出されます。

*センシビリティ

*sensibilities

Software applications exist independently inside the Mac. By manipulating the Mac, you can open and utilize these applications, bringing the Mac to life. You can't do anything without applications, but you can bring them up, combine them, and put them to work. By going to work on the Mac and using one's own sensibilities, individual talent can be brought forth within the confines of the computer environment.

大英博物館で絵を描く学生・ロンドン 1992
Students painting in British Museum. London, 1992

W ● Macって、誰が作ったの？
ho created the Mac?

人類最初のコンピュータ、ENIAC（エニャック・電子計算機）が1946年に発明され、コンピュータ時代の幕開けとなりました。やがて30年の歳月が過ぎ、カリフォルニアに住むスティーブ・ウォズニアクとスティーブ・ジョブズが、世界で初めてのパーソナル・コンピュータ（パソコン）を発明しました。「誰でも自由に使えるコンピュータを世の中の人に広めたい」と、２人は1977年春、アップル社を設立しました。アップルII、アップルIIe、アップルIIc、アップルIIGSと進化を続け現在に至ります。

*パーソナル・コンピュータ

*personal computer

Mankind's first computer was the ENIAC (Electronic Computing Machine) developed in 1946 and heralding the start of the computer age. More than thirty years later, in California, Steve Wosniac and Steve Jobs built the first personal computer. With the pledge to "Give the world a computer anyone can use," the two founded Apple Computer in the Spring of 1977. Beginning with the Apple II, Apple IIe, Apple IIc and Apple IIGS, the computer has evolved into its present form.

Apple II, 1977

W●デジタルとアナログはどう違うの？
What is the difference between digital and analog?

『虹』ステコン技法 1992
"Rainbow" Stacom method, 1992

デジタルとアナログという言葉がよく使われます。デジタル・コンピュータは（電算）計数型コンピュータ（データを離散的な数値、特に０と１との組み合わせで表現し処理する電子計算機）で、アナログ・コンピュータは（電算）情報を連続的な量で表して処理するコンピュータです。つまりデジタルは計数型で、アナログは連続的な量の意味を指し、ここでは手で描くことをアナログ、Macで描くことをデジタルと言います。

The terms digital and analog are often heard. A digital computer (calculating machine) performs by assigning numbers - in particular 0s and 1s - to pieces of data, an analog computer by managing data as a continuous calculation. In short, a digital computer calculates, while an analog computer connects. For our purposes, drawing by hand is analog, drawing by a machine is digital.

『軽業師』7点シリーズの1点
多摩美術大学卒業制作:秋山孝 1979
"The Little Pilgrim" first of 7-part series.
Takashi Akiyama, Tama Art University, 1979

W●イラストレーションにおけるテクノロジーって、なに？
What is illustration technology?

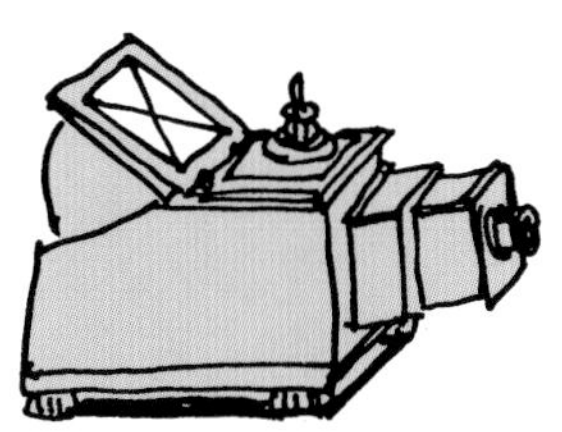

カメラ・オブスクーラ・スケッチ:秋山孝 1993
Camera obscura. Sketch by Takashi Akiyama, 1933

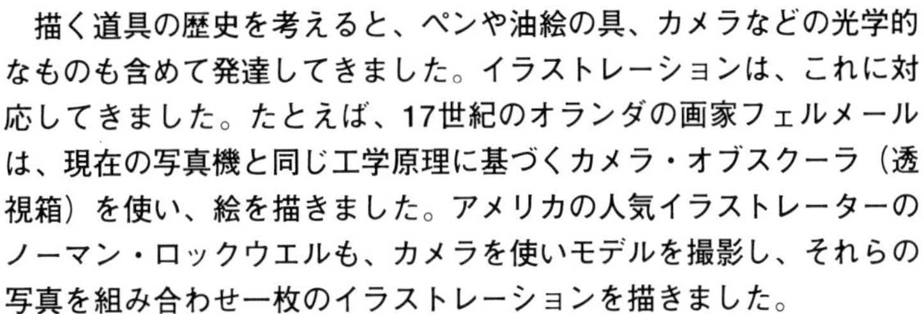

描く道具の歴史を考えると、ペンや油絵の具、カメラなどの光学的なものも含めて発達してきました。イラストレーションは、これに対応してきました。たとえば、17世紀のオランダの画家フェルメールは、現在の写真機と同じ工学原理に基づくカメラ・オブスクーラ（透視箱）を使い、絵を描きました。アメリカの人気イラストレーターのノーマン・ロックウエルも、カメラを使いモデルを撮影し、それらの写真を組み合わせ一枚のイラストレーションを描きました。

つまり、カメラの出現でイラストレーターも写真技術をビジュアルコミュニケーションの表現のために、補助的技術として自分の表現の中に取り入れました。

*ビジュアルコミュニケーション

ぼくの場合は、レンズを通し拡大された線を使い、イラストレーションの表現として自分の中にテクノロジーを取り入れました。つまり、テクノロジーの発達に伴って自分がみえてきました。Macがでてきたときも、同じように表現の広がりとして、ぼくの中にスーッと入り込んできたのです。

*テクノロジー

Thinking of the development of illustrating implements, one must include everything from pens and paint to cameras and photo technology. Illustration has developed in response to these tools. For instance, in 17th century Holland the painter Jan Vermmer used the camera obscura, which was based on the same principles as the modern camera, to create his art. And the popular American illustrator Norman Rockwell used a camera to photograph different models for his drawings, which were composites.

In other words, the camera has been used by illustrators as a supporting technology in their visual communication work.

*visual communication work

I have used camera lenses to magnify lines for my illustrations, taking this technology into my work and making it a part of myself. By understanding new technology which has developed one comes to better see oneself. Likewise, with the advent of the Mac, I have expanded my expressive capacity by making it completely a part of myself.

* technology

W ● DTPって、なに？ hat is DTP?

1987年頃、話題になりはじめたのがDTP（ディスクトップ・パブリッシング）で、パソコンを使って誰でもが簡単に卓上で編集・出版ができるようになりました。あくまでも、出版分野の話だったのが、グラフィックデザインの分野でも十分使えるシステムになりました。

これからは、いつでも誰でも本が作れるし、デザインができるようになりました。センスさえあれば、神秘的なデザイナーがやってきた仕事がそんなに難しいことではなくなってきました。経済原則と情報のスピードのふたつがそうさせています。ローコストで速いという二大原則があるかぎり、いまのところストップさせる思想がでてこないから、あるところまでいくでしょう。DTPは1450年のグーテンベルクの活版印刷の発明以来の偉大なシステムといえます。

*グーテンベルク

*Gutenberg

Around 1987, the term DTP (Desktop Publishing) came into use, referring to the ability of anyone with a personal computer to easily edit and publish from their own desk. Originally, this system was used primarily in publishing, but recently it has become applicable to the graphic design field as well.

Now anyone can make a book or design. Anyone with sense can create the once mystifying work of the graphic designer without great difficulty. Economic laws and the speed of information have made both possible. And there seems to be no end in sight to the increase of speed and the reduction of cost. Since the invention of the typeface by Gutenberg in 1450, DTP has become a great system indeed.

42行聖書 1453年ころ
The 42 column Bible, c. 1453

● コンピュータはイラストレーションでも万能なの？
Is the computer really all-powerful in illustration?

コンピュータが万能だと思っていること自体、みょうな感じがしますが、いまだにコンピュータはなんでもできると思っている人がいます。その原因は、コンピュータの販売宣伝戦略やコミックスのビジュアルでの表現における、なんでもできるというイメージで洗脳されているからです。しかもとても便利でキーボードを軽くたたくと、ロボットがまるで人間のように働いてくれるように思っています。

*ロボット
*robot

しかし手で描いたりするよりは、はるかに時間がかかり、当たり前の作業をもくもくとするデジタル的忍耐力が必要です。つまり、時間がたっぷりかかります。だけど、デジタルの魅力は、一度記憶したものに関しては風化したり、劣化したりは決してしません。それは、コンピュータの特徴である、秩序や整理することに対しての非常な能力を発揮するからです。たとえば、記憶したものを呼び出したりしながら、新たな組合せや合成、変換などイラストレーションにおいて、その作品をいつまでも新鮮に活用できます。

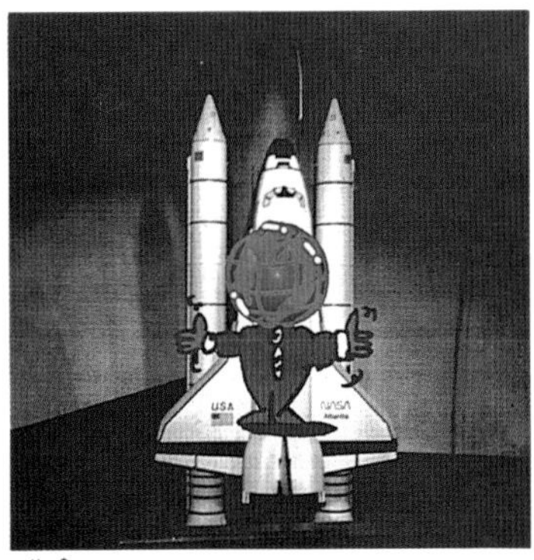

『時代』ステコン技法 1991
"Age" Stacom method, 1991

Thinking about the capabilities of the computer makes me feel a bit odd. There are people who believe that anything can be done on the computer. The cause of this misapprehension is probably the marketing strategies of computer sellers and comics, who project the image that anything can done on a computer just by hitting the convenient keyboard and letting the robot take over.

In fact, drawing with a computer can be much more tedious than drawing by hand. Digital illustrating requires a special degree of patience, and lots of time. But the advantages are that in computer illustrating, once a work has been entered into memory, one need never worry about it disintegrating or wearing down. Moreover, the specialty of the computer is its ability to reorder and arrange things. In this area it is nearly all-powerful. Just call up any work from memory; you can recombine and synthesize and alter it in any way you wish, recreating it afresh every time.

W ● ステコン技法って、なに？
hat is the "stacom" method?

ぼくは、はじめてMacのモニターの発光体をみたとき、あまりの美しさに感動しました。ヨーロッパのステンドグラスの美しさに似ていると思いました。光、色、形から受ける感動は、絵の具の色よりも強烈でした。

*ステンドグラス

ステンドグラスに透過された光の美しさは、フランスのシャルトル大聖堂を代表に、12世紀ゴシック建築様式の中で花開きました。この色の輝きは、光を反射して知覚するあらゆる絵画技法の色彩にはるかにまさるものがあります。それは、ここを訪れる人の神秘的幻想を、美的感動を持って表現しているかのように思えます。この神なる光は、現代の我々にとっても、今だなお衰えることなく聖なる空間を支配しています。

20世紀末（ラスト・ディケイド）になって電子メディアは、ますます私達に新しい視覚の体験をあたえ続けています。

*20世紀末（ラスト・ディケイド）

*電子メディア

ぼくにとって、コンピュータのモニターは、まさにステンドグラス技法を垣間みる思いがします。これらのイメージからできるイラストレーションなどを総称して、秋山孝のステコン技法（ステンドグラス・コンピュータ技法）と呼んでいます。

The first time I saw an image on a Mac monitor I was overwhelmed by the beauty of the light. The light and color and form reminded me of the beauty of European stained glass windows. The color of the monitor seemed much more powerful than a picture.

Stained glass, as exemplified in the French Cathedral of Chartres, was developed along with Gothic architecture in the 12th century. In its sparkling color and reflected light it far exceeds the beauty of any form of painting. The mysterious visions and aesthetic expression of the people who visit these gothic places are all expressed here. These godlike images of glass still dominate our modern holy places.

ドゥオーモ・ミラノ 1992
Duomo. Milan, 1992

And now, in the last decade of the twentieth century, electronic media continues to bring us new visual experiences.

For myself, the computer monitor offers an eternal stained glass method. The icons, born of deflected light, are the obvious symbols. All of my illustrations, built of these images, I name the Akiyama Takashi stacom (stained glass) computer method.

*stained glass

*last decade of the twentieth century

*electronic media

W ●どうして、Macでイラストレーションを描くの？
Why do you illustrate on a Mac?

*線

ぼくは線の研究をしてきました。筆の線、ペンの線、マーカーの線、引っかいた線、エッチングの線、リトグラフの線などいろいろな線を見てきました。

線の成り立ちは、たとえば、インクの場合は紙の繊維の中にインクが染み込んで出来る線。鉛筆やコンテの場合は、紙の繊維の中に引っかかって粒子がのってできる線。線には必ず濃淡があるのだけれど、

*ドット（点の集合）

コンピュータのデジタルの線はドット（点の集合）であって均一です。根本的に違います。

1989年ニューヨークの美術大学に行った時、家庭の事情で学校に行けない子供たちが描いたMacの展覧会がありました。そのときにプリントアウトされたものが、展示してありました。それをみた時、愕然としました。なぜなら、今まで人間が引いてきた線と全く違う線だったからです。見たことのない線でした。それは均一でした。これは、偉大な発見であり偉大な表現だと思いました。たとえば、人間が描いた白黒の線をハイコントラストで複写して、印画紙に焼き付けた線に近い。人間の持っている息吹きや、息づかいがまったくありません。これは、線に興味のあるぼくにとって、不思議な魅力的な線だったので、Macでイラストレーションを描きたいと思いました。ドットで出てくるギザギザな感じも新鮮でした。

*lines

I have researched lines - lines of the pencil, the pen, the marker; etchings, lithographs, scratches. I have looked at all kinds of lines.

Lines are composed in various ways. For instance, lines of ink are formed by ink dyeing the fiber of the paper. With pencil and conte, scratches are made in the fiber, and particles are left behind. All hand drawn lines are of uneven thickness. Not so with

*groups of dots

digital computer lines, which are created with groups of dots, and always evenly - a basic difference between the two methods.

In 1989, in New York, I saw an exhibit of works created on Mac by children who could not attend school because of family problems. Exhibited were printouts of these works. I was stunned. What I saw was lines completely different form anything so far drawn by the human hand. Lines never seen before. They were all evenly drawn. It was a great discovery of great works. They resembled, for example, black and white lines reproduced in high contrast, as if on Photostat paper. They didn't seem to breathe like normal human works. For myself, as a student of the line, they were something totally strange and attractive. This is when I first realized a desire to draw with the Mac. The zig-zag creations of the dot were utterly fresh to my eye.

子供のためのコンピュータルーム
シカゴ科学産業博物館 1983
Children's Computer Room.
Museum of Science and Industry, Chicago, 1983

W ●なぜ、コンピュータの線と人間の引く線は違うの？
hy are computer lines and lines drawn by hand different?

定規で引く線は、定規という与えられた補助道具で引いた線です。人間が引いた線は、人間の腕力の差や手首の癖によって、個人の差が出てきますが、コンピュータの場合は筆跡鑑定が不可能です。マウスで描いたものは、誰が描いたか判りません。線における個人のオリジナリティは明快だと思っていましたが、共有することが出来る線ができました。誰が引いても同じ線ができます。言葉で描ける線。つまり、「何ミリの太さで何センチの線をA点からB点まで引く」と入力できます。誰でも同じ線が引けます。機能や機械の違いはでますが個人の違いはでません。

*言葉で描ける線

たとえば、建築図面などは共有する線がいい。自分が描いたものをつぎの人に客観的にコミュニケーションするために、コンピュータを使えば使うほど、正しくコミュニケーションできます。ところが、線の中には想像をして欲しいものもあります。それによってムードだとか情緒だとかを伝えたい時もあります。

A line drawn with a ruler is one created with a supplementary tool - a ruler. Lines drawn by hand are created with the strength of the arm and the habits of the hand, and therefore express individuality. But no one can analyze the handwriting of a computer. Lines drawn with a mouse cannot be ascribed to any given individual; though the lines may seem clearly original, more lines can be added by another hand which fit them perfectly. No one can tell the difference. These are lines written with words. You can command the computer to drawn a line of X thickness between points A and B. Anyone can draw the same line. Differences in machinery and functions may be apparent, but not human individuality.

*lines written with words

For instance, consider the lines of an architectural design. By using a computer, you can accurately communicate your ideas to the viewer. The more you rely on the computer, the more perfect the communication. But beware; there are also times when you want to express mood and feeling.

自宅図面・秋山孝 1993
Author's home. Takashi Akiyama, 1993

W●なぜ、コンピュータでもデッサンは必要なの？
Why is design necessary in the computer?

今までぼくがMacを扱う人を見ていて思うのは、コンピュータはあくまでも道具であって、その道具をどう利用するかとか、その人の考え方だとかに大きく左右されるということです。特にデザインワークやイラストレーションを描く時に、その人なりの造形的能力が問われます。その造形的能力の基準は非常に難しいが、今まで絵を描くときに必要であった形や動き、構図、量、空間などは、デッサンでもかなり重要な表現のエレメントでした。

コンピュータもソフトの中にいろいろな機能が入っているのだけれど、その機能をどのように活かしていくかが大切です。厳しい造形的なセンスが必要です。従来のデッサンやクロッキーなどは、脳と手と目と体で感じるものも含めたものが、絵を描く時に必要でした。コンピュータでイラストレーションを描くことにおいても、デッサンのトレーニングは必要です。しかしデッサンだけではだめで、総合的にいろいろな見地からみた造形的なセンスをみがいた上でコンピュータを使うと、いままでにない考え方と表現が出てきます。

*造形的なセンス

*strict formal sense

『セントジョセフ』
学生時代の石膏デッサン:秋山孝 1975
"St. Joseph" Design of Stone sculpture, Takashi Akiyama, 1975

Until now the computer has been utilized entirely as a tool by its users, and one can see the very different ways in which individual thinking has determined the computer's use. Especially in design, and in illustrations, one can see the creative energy of the individual. The basis of this creative energy is difficult to explain, but the required elements are the same as in painting - form and movement, structure, quantity, space, etc.

There are various functions contained in computer software; the important question is how to use them. Strict formal sense is required. All the designs and drafts you have created hitherto, and the senses of your mind, eyes, hands and body, are essential to your work. In computer illustration, design training is essential. But design elements alone are not enough; a comprehensive grasp and polished sense of all aspects of form will lead you to new ways of expression when you take up the computer.

W ●なぜ、Macと絵画の質感（マチエール）は違うの？
hy are the textures of computer works and paintings different?

コンピュータの場合、画面やプリントアウトしたものは、デジタル信号で出てきます。コンピュータでのテクスチャーマッピングという技法による表現は、写真と同じような質感に近い。ところが、アナログの油絵や水彩画、日本画は、マチエールがでてきます。それぞれが持っている独特な素材感が語る凹凸があります。油絵の具の質感、木の質感、土の質感、錆びの質感、いろいろな質感を考えると、Macの質感はコンピュータからでてくる質感であって、絵画のような質感は絶対にでません。その違いを認識し、それぞれが持っている独自性を考えて、コンピュータの質感をオリジナルとして考えればいいわけです。

*質感

*quality

In computers, screens and printouts are created with digital information. The computer technique of texture mapping offers a quality close to that of film. But in analog work such as water and oil painting, or Japanese painting, the material is different. Each has its own individual texture and surface variation. These various textures - of the tools of oil painting, wood, earth, rust, etc. - can in no way be rendered on a Mac. Each medium must be explored within its own limitations, and this includes the computer. Consider the unique possibilities of the computer and develop your own innovations.

『風景』秋山孝 1978
"Scene" Takashi Akiyama, 1978

W ●アナログとデジタルの融合って、なに？
hat is meant by the fusion of analog and digital?

アナログデザインとデジタルデザインそれぞれをめざすデザイナーの間で、お互いに考え方の相違において、ぶつかり合う場面に出くわすことがありました。お互いを否定し合うことは、ぼくにとってナンセンスな議論に思えます。そこで、アナログとデジタルの融合をどのようにしたらはかれるでしょうか。それぞれの持っている特徴を分析し、いかに活かすかを考えました。その中で、特にイラストレーターの立場で描くことをデジタルデザインの中に導入しました。

新たな表現を模索する必要性を感じ、DDP（デジタルデザイン&プリプレス）やDTP（ディスクトップ・パブリッシング）という考え方の中で、イラストレーションの果たす役割の必然性を発見したいという欲望がありました。

『ALIEN』ステコン技法・コピック+デジタル 1992
"ALIEN" Stacom method, Copic+Digital, 1992

アナログとデジタルの融合は、システムをつくることとイラストレーションのデジタルデータ化を進めることによって、可能なシミュレーションとデザインの新たなる展開を見せます。

*デジタルデータ化

There is opportunity for collision between digital and analog design, and I see no reason to pay attention to nonsensical debate between the opposing camps. The question is how to fuse the digital and analog approaches. I have thought of the features of each method, and tried to hit upon ways to use both. The most obvious is the introduction of illustrations into digital design.

Feeling the need to discover new elements of expression, I have sought to discover in DDP (digital design and pre-press) and DTP the full applicability of illustration.

*creation of digital data banks

Through the combination of digital and analog methods, and by the creation of systems and digital data banks, I have discovered new possibilities in simulation and design.

W●イラストレーションって、なに？ hat is an illustration?

*もうひとつの言葉

*視覚化

イラストレーションとは、ビジュアルを通して伝達するもうひとつの言葉です。視覚化されたもののほうが、従来の文字で書かれたものよりも説得力を持つこともあります。ということは、イラストレーションというのは、言葉では言い表せないもの、言葉を超えてしまっているものを絵で表現することです。それはイラストレーションの役割でもあります。

*コミュニケーション

人間のコミュニケーションの方法には、いろいろな方法がありますが、文字を含めて言葉による方法と、視覚に訴える方法のふたつが、主なものです。イラストレーションは、言葉では伝えることのできないものを伝えることができます。あるいは言葉よりも、より能率的に伝えることができます。言葉の補助手段では決してありません。

*another term for illustration

*changed into something visual

Another term for illustration might be communication through the visual. And that which has been changed into something visual is more persuasive than that which is written in words. Thus illustration is something which cannot be expressed in words, which in fact goes beyond words. And that is the role of illustration.

*communication

Humans possess various forms of communication, including the two major forms, i.e. text and language, and visual expressions. Illustration conveys ideas which words cannot; or rather, conveys them more efficiently than words. Illustration is never a mere supplement to language.

『握手』 イラストレーション:秋山孝 1990

"Handshake" Takashi Akiyama illustration, 1990

Chapter
2

W ● Macのそれぞれの呼び名は？
hat are the terms for a Mac?

Macを通してコミュニケーションするにはそれぞれの呼び名を知らなければなりません。ここでは、ぼくのMacくんに主な呼び名と説明をつけました。が、もっとも代表的なところをわかりやすくつけただけですべてではありません。それぞれの持っている機種のマニュアルを参考にしてください。

In order to use a Mac for communication, a knowledge of the names of the parts is necessary. Here I've labeled some of the parts of my Mac, but this is far from all. For a full explanation of all the parts and their functions please refer to your manuals.

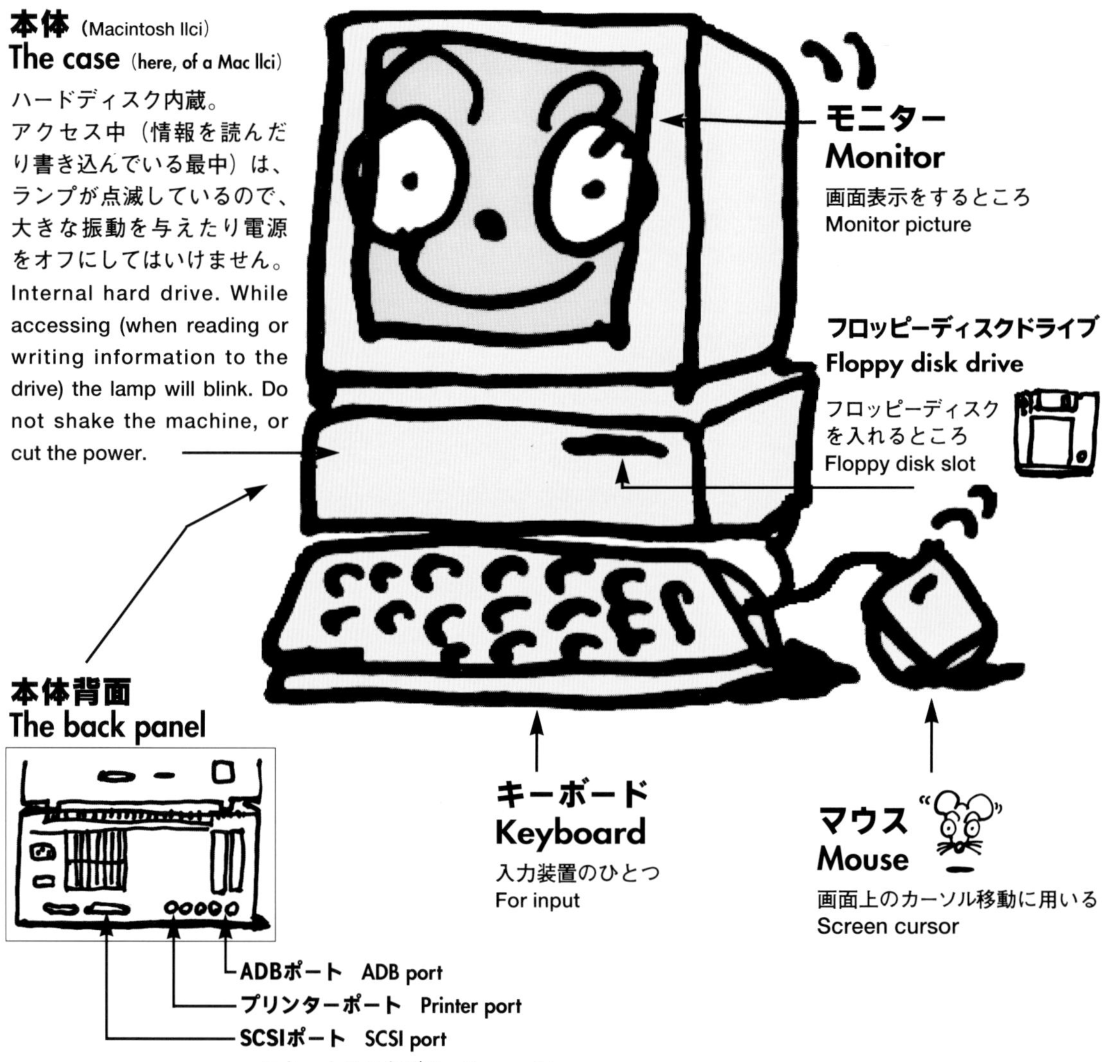

W● なぜ、Macはこんなに使いやすいの？
Why is the Mac so easy to use?

他のパソコンと違うところは、マウスとアイコンとプルダウンメニューで操作するところです。さらに説明すれば、Macを立ち上げたとき最初に現われる、あのゴミ箱のあるデスクトップ（DeskTop …卓上）の画面とメニューバー（アッププル・マークの並び）です。それは、コンピュータを抑制しているオペレーティング・システムや、コマンドに悩まされることなく、このデスクトップで操作できる環境にあります。

What makes the Mac different from other PCs are its mouse, icons and pulldown menus. One might add to these the desktop itself, which is seen at start-up and includes the "Trash" pail and Menu Bar (where the apple mark is seen.) This is the environment through which you enter the Mac operating system, free from worries about complicated commands.

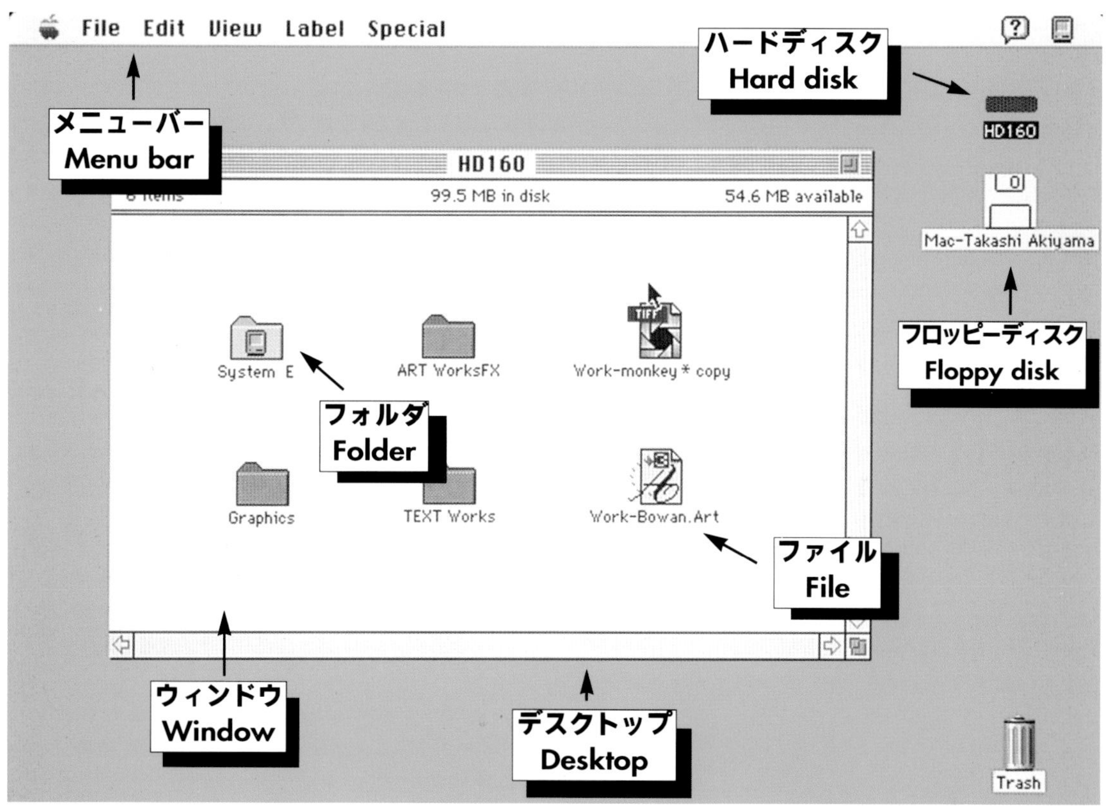

マウス■ Mouse
Macの操作はマウスとキーボードでします。
マウスは英語でねずみという意味。
The Mac is operated with the mouse and keyboard.

マウスの使い方■How to use the mouse.
クリック…ボタンを1回押す。
ダブルクリック…ボタンを2回押す。
ドラッグ…ボタンを押したまま移動する。
Click...push the button once.
Double-click....push the button twice.
Drag...moving with the button depressed.

アイコン■ Icon
Macの画面に出ている絵のこと。この絵を見れば、どこに目指すソフトウエアがあるか一目でわかります。

The term for the pictures that appear on the Mac screen. With these pictures you immediately "see" the application you are seeking.

プルダウンメニュー■Pulldown menu
画面の一番上に表示されているメニューです。マウスを押すことによってメニューの一覧が下方向に引きだされます。

The menu is displayed at the very top Click the mouse to open the column below each function.

W ●ソフトって、なに？
hat is software?

ソフトウエアのことで、コンピュータ本体の機械部分をハードウエアと呼ぶのに対して、コンピュータに演算などをさせるプログラムなどの技術の総称です。Macの環境において、絵を作成・編集するグラフィックソフトは、ワードプロセッサと同じように重要です。ここではグラフィックソフトの流れを概観し、Macイラスト講座の基本ともいうべきソフトの選択方法について触れてみたいと思います。

Unlike hardware, which includes all the machine parts in your computer, software is the program, or written instructions, which make your computer perform tasks. When creating or editing art in the Mac environment your graphic software has the same importance as a word processor. Shown below is the graphic software used in Getting Started as a Mac Illustrator, along with comments on what types of software you may want to use.

3Ｄツール■3D tools

３次元イメージを生成するために使われるグラフィックソフトです。StrataVision 3d、レンダリングモジュールで有名なものがRenderManといったところです。

This graphic software enables you to make 3D images. StrataVision 3D, and Render Man, which is popular in model rendering, are two well-known programs.

アニメーションツール■Animation tools

動く絵を作成するためのソフトです。MacroMind Directorはペイントツールに勝るとも劣らないフルカラーグラフィックソフトを内蔵しています。Studio/１はモノクロのアニメーションを作成するソフトです。

Software that enables you to make a picture move. MacroMind Director is a full-color graphic soft which I use. Studio/1 is a good application for monochrome animation.

ペイントツール■Paint tools

ペイント系（グラフィック）ソフトともいい、最終的にドットで絵が描かれます。代表的なソフトはMacPaintやPixelPaint 、Studio/32などで、Adobe Photoshopのようなフォトレタッチソフトもあります。

Painting software, also known as paint soft, basically builds pictures with dots. The most famous applications are ones like MacPaint, PixelPaint and Studio/32, with Adobe Photoshop useful for font retouching.

ドローツール■Drawing tools

ドロー系（グラフィック）ソフトともいい、絵はドットの集合体ではなく、数学的図形データを視覚化したものです。代表的なソフトとしては、MacDrawがあげられます。

Drawing soft does not build pictures with dots; rather, it visually renders dimensional data. One popular application is MacDraw .

ポストスクリプトグラフィックツール■Postscript graphic tools

ポストスクリプト系（グラフィック）ソフトともいい、ドローツールに含まれるグラフィックソフトです。ポストスクリプトのベジェ曲線（解説 p.34）を画面上で操作・編集することができます。今までは雲型定規を使ってしか描けなかった複雑なイラストも描くことができます。Adobe IllustratorやAldus FreeHandなどがあります。

Also called postscript soft, these graphic applications include drawing tools. They allow you to manipulate and edit postscript bezier curves on the screen (see p.34). Cloud shapes, and other complex shapes which must otherwise drawn by hand, can be created easily with Adobe Illustrator and Aldus FreeHand.

A ● グラフィックソフトの系譜
graphic soft tree.

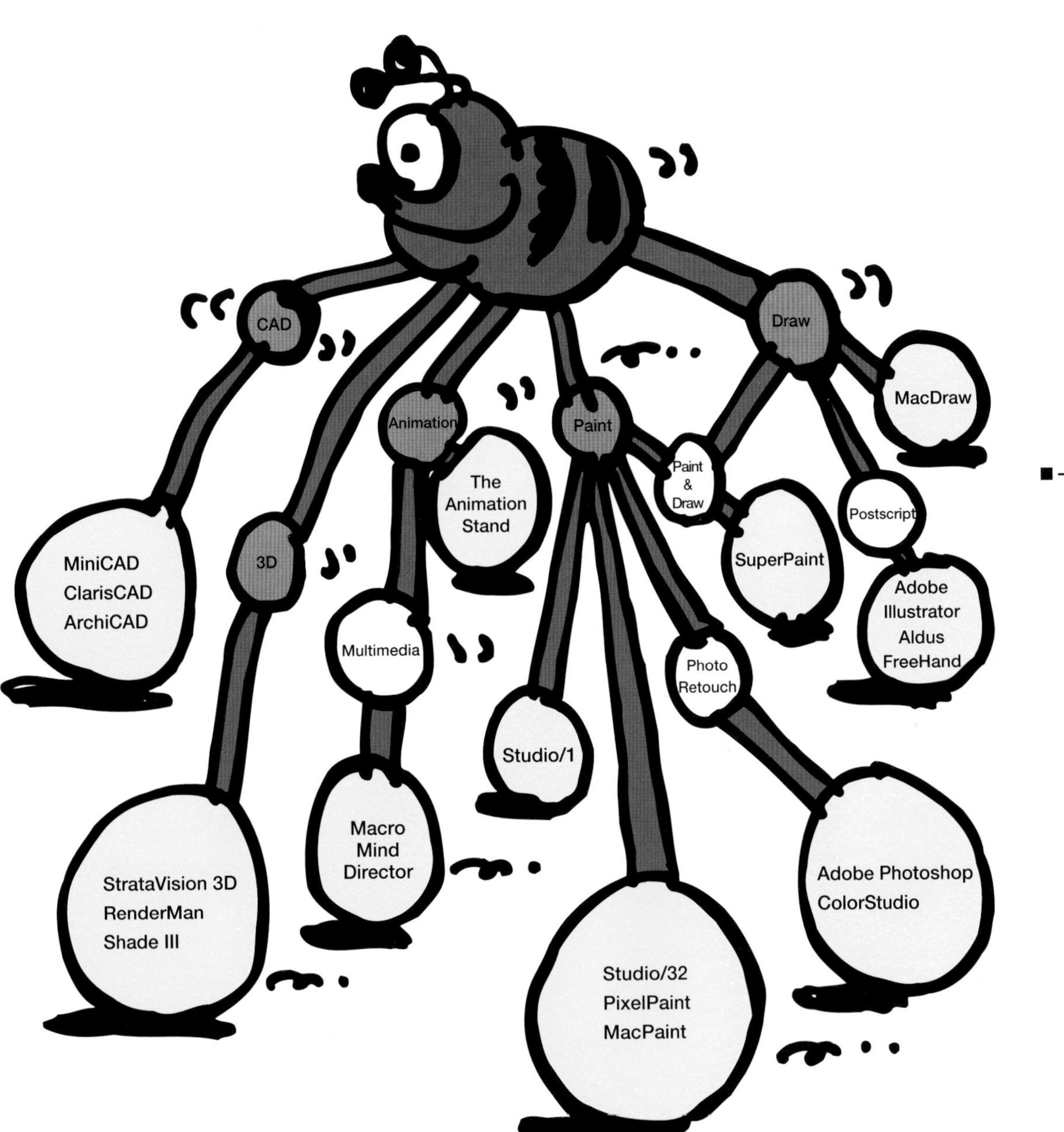

W● 人間の手で描けないことって、なに？
What is drawing without the human hand?

太古の昔から人間は､視覚に訴える力を使って自分の考えや夢を伝えてきました。そのためには必ず描くための道具が必要でした。それを考えると､誰もが原始人が描いている姿を思い起こしたりするでしょう。ひっかいたり擦ったりして、なんとか自分の伝えたいイメージを形として表現しました。ところが、人間の描くための技術は、道具とともに発達してきました。現代は表現技術が急激に発達し、新たな視覚のコミュニケーションができるようになりました。その最たるものが、コンピュータで描く表現のように思われます。それは、私たちの脳に浮かぶイメージをキーボードやマウスを通して、デジタル表現の力を借りて可能になったわけです。つまり、人間の手で描くことが困難なことをいとも簡単にできるようになりました。たとえば、限りなく精度の高い幾何学的表現がそれです。

Since prehistoric times humans have used the power of sight to communicate their thoughts and dreams. For this they have needed tools with which to draw. This idea leads us to imagine the primitive man in the act of drawing. Whether by scratching or rubbing, this individual attempted to express form and image. Early man's ability to draw evolved together with the development of drawing tools. Today, highly advanced tools enable us to create superior forms of visual communication. The most advanced tool of expression is the computer. We use the mouse and keyboard, and borrow digital power, to produce the images in our minds. Now the difficulty of drawing by hand has been removed. For instance, a geometric shape of high precision is now within our grasp.

制作プロセス■Production Process
Adobe Illustrator 3.2を使って、直線で図形を描きます。
※ペンツールは、クリックした点を結びながら線を描きます。
Drawing straight lines with Adobe Illustrator 3.2.
※Click the pen tool at each point to connect the lines.

1. ペンツールを選びます。直線の始点をクリックします。（カーソルは×から＋に）
   Select the pen tool. Click the starting point of the straight line. (Move the cursor from x to +)

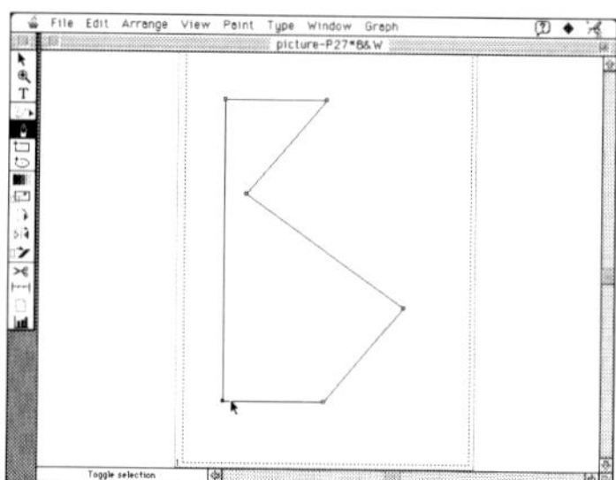

2. 次の場所をクリックします。Shift＋クリックで垂直線が引かれます。最後に始点のアンカーポイントをクリックすると、多角形（クローズパス）を描くことができます。
   Click the next place. Use Shift+Click to draw straight vertical lines.Finally, click the starting "anchor" point to finish the many-cornered (cross perspective) shape.

3. 色をつけるオブジェクトを選びます。「ペイント」メニューで線の太さ、図形の色を決めます。ダイアログボックスの「塗りつぶし」「線の設定」で設定します。
   Select an object for coloring. Set the line thickness and object color under the "Paint Style" menu. Dialogue boxes will appear for "Fil" and "Stroke."

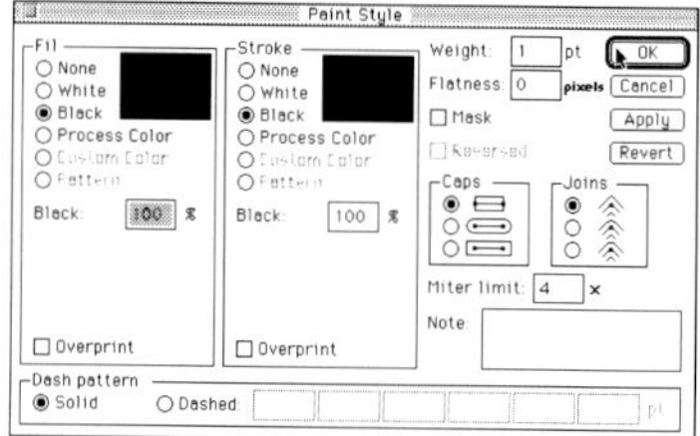

W ● マウスで描くって、なに？ hat is drawing with the mouse?

ぼくにとって、マウスで描いた経験はとても不思議な感覚のものでした。ディズニーランドのスターツアーズにのったような体験でした。それは、実体験を通したものではなくシミュレーションだったのです。モニターの中で仮想現実を描くことは、今までにないとても楽しい表現の喜びを覚えるものでした。

For me, drawing with the mouse has been a very strange experience. It's like riding the "Star Tours" at Tokyo Disneyland. Not a real tour, but a simulation tour. The happy hypothetical shapes in the monitor have been a pleasure to create.

制作プロセス■Production Process

Adobe Photoshop 2.0を使って、線を描きます。
※ブラシツールは、選択したブラシの形そのままにペイントできます。
Drawing lines with Adobe Photoshop 2.0.
※The brush tool can be used just as it is for painting.

1. ブラシツールを選びます。ブラシツールアイコンをダブルクリック（またはOption＋クリック）するとオプション指定のダイアログが表示されます。

   Choose the brush tool. Double click on the brush tool icon (or use Option+Click) to bring up option dialogue box.

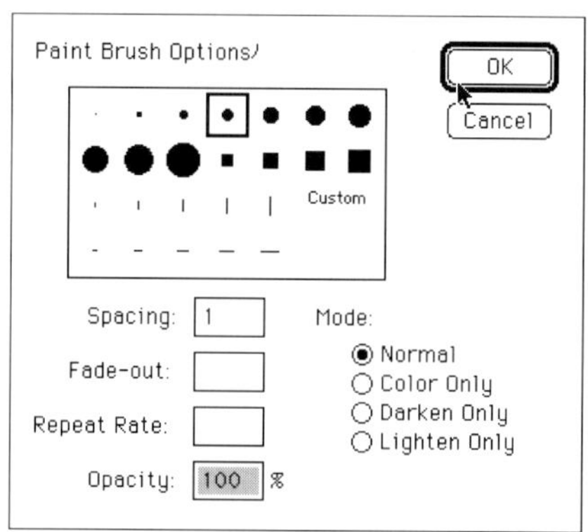

2. 好みの大きさと形を選んで、それぞれの線を選んで描きます。

   Select and draw various lines.

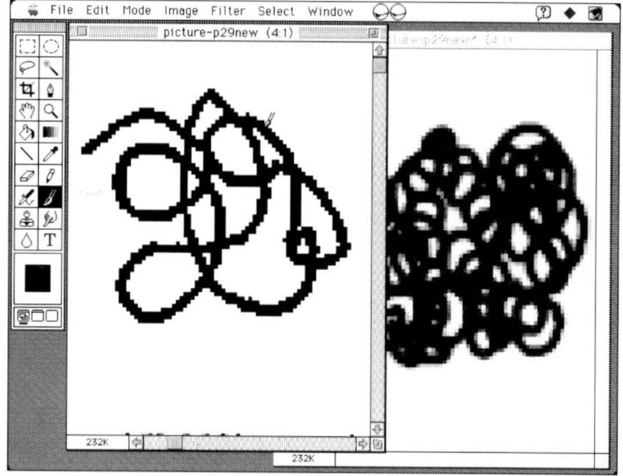

D● ドットで描いてみたい?
o you want to draw with dots?

表現の始まりは、ドット（点）です。そのつぎに線があり、面があります。コンピュータの線も点の集合でそれが連続してできたものです。つまり、ドットは造形の大切なエレメントとしてぼくらに訴えかけます。Macでは、この造形エレメントは容易につくれ表現できます。ドットの表現のバリエーションは、とても美しくて「Macイラスト講座」の基本です。

The beginning of expression is the dot. After that comes the line, then the surface. These are creations of the consecutive dots and lines coming from the computer. Dots are the most important building element. On the computer, it is easy to produce works from the dot. The various expressions of the dot are the beautiful basis of "Getting Started as a Mac Illustrator."

制作プロセス■Production Process
Adobe Photoshop 2.0を使って、ドット（点）で描きます。
※鉛筆ツールは、選択した鉛筆の形そのままにペイントできます。
Drawing dots with Adobe Photoshop 2.0.
※You can even paint with the pencil tool without changing its shape.

1. 鉛筆ツールを選びます。ツールアイコンをダブルクリックするとオプション設定のダイアログが表示されます。鉛筆の大きさと形を選択します。不透明度を100%～1%の範囲で指定します。

   Choose the pencil tool. Double click on the tool icon to bring up the option dialogue box. Choose the size and thickness of your pencil. Set transparency anywhere from 1-100%.

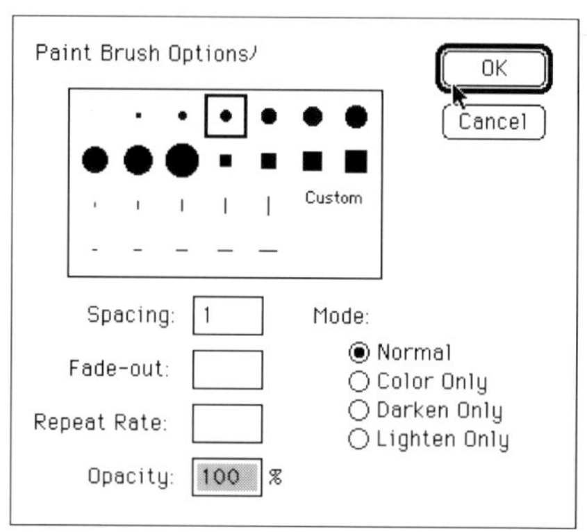

2. クリックします。鉛筆の大きさと形と不透明度を変更しクリックします。

   Click the mouse. By clicking you can change the size of the pencil and the degree of transparency.

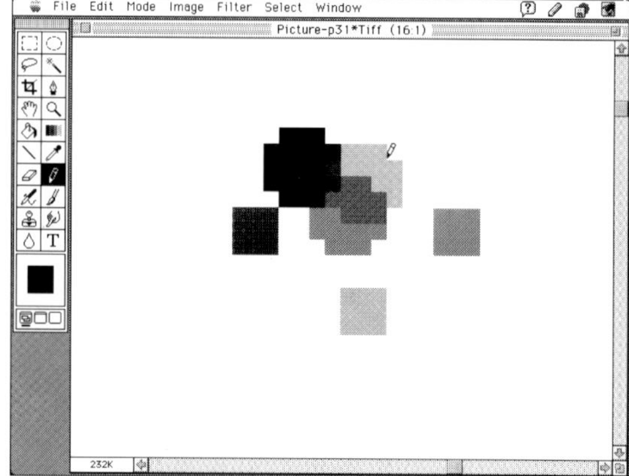

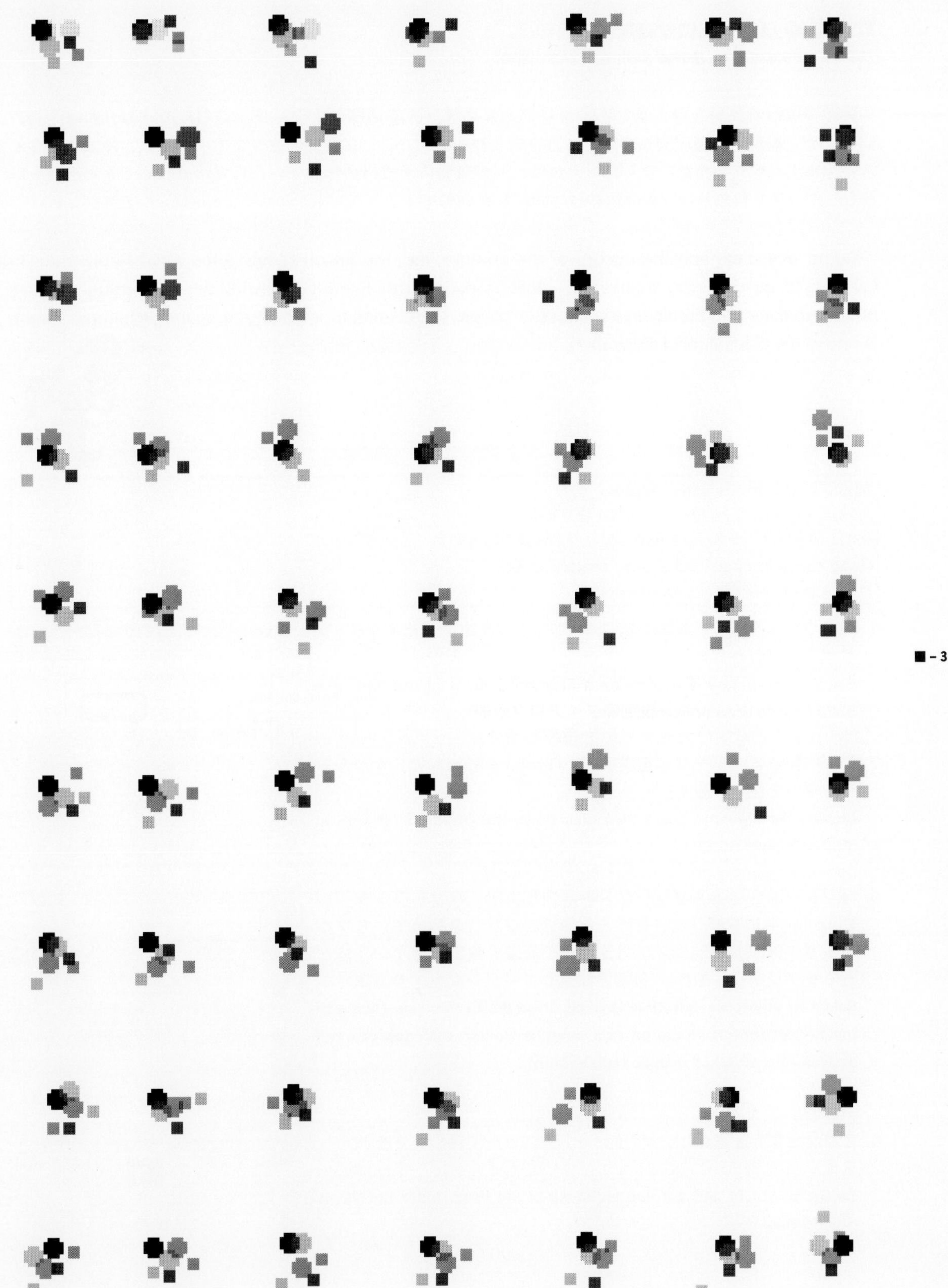

W ● 直線でなにが表現できるの？
hat can be created with a straight line?

直線の造形の歴史を考えると、イタリア・ルネサンスに活躍したウッチェロ（Paolo Uccello 1397-1475）が、幾何学や透視図法に熱中し数々の名作を生んだことにさかのぼります。そこに、直線でできる透視図による空間を発見しました。それは、絵の裏側にある構造体です。ここでは直線でできる空間を理解し、イラストレーションの表現のひとつにしたいのです。

Going way back into the history of the straight line, the Italian renaissance artist Paolo Uccello (1397-1475) used lines to create many masterpieces of transparent geometric design. Through the use of lines in diagrams he discovered interior space. Using lines to suggest the space within a structure is one of the chief aims of illustration.

制作プロセス■Production Process
Adobe Illustrator 3.2を使って、直線を描きます。
※ペンツールは、クリックした点を結びながら線を描きます。
Using Adobe Illustrator 3.2 to draw straight lines.
※Click to connect lines between points.

1. ペンツールを選び、直線の始点をクリックします。Shift＋クリックで水平線が引かれます。
Choose the pencil and click on the starting point of the line. Use Shift+Click to draw horizontal lines.

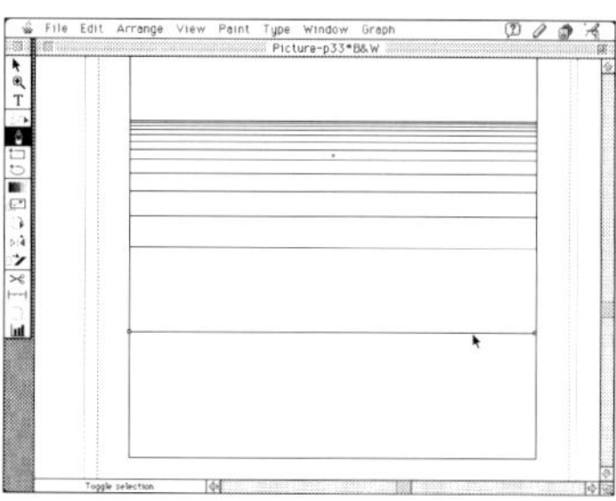

2. コピーするオブジェクトを選択し、Option＋Shiftを押しながらドラッグして移動します。
Choose the object to copy, then hold down the Option+Shift keys to drag to desired position.

3. リフレクトさせるオブジェクトを選択します。リフレクトツールでOptionキーを押しながら軸となる点をクリックします。リフレクトダイアログボックスが開きます。角度の設定を行ない「コピー」をクリックします。（数値を設定してリフレクトする方法）
Select an object for reflection. Holding down the Option key, click with the Reflect tool to create an axis point. A Reflect dialogue box will appear. After setting the angle click to copy.

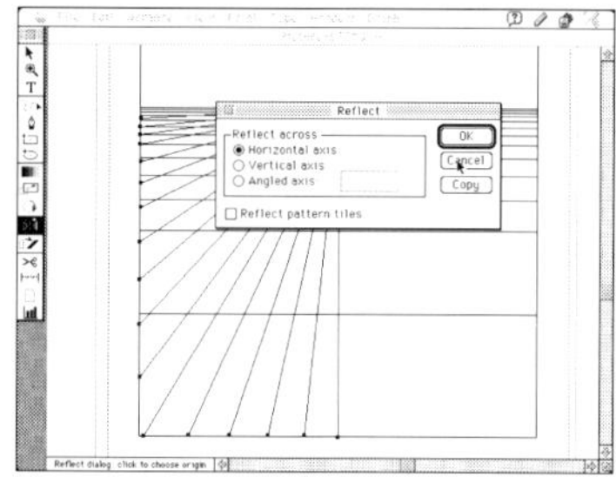

4. オブジェクトを選択し、「ペイント」メニューで線の太さを設定します。
Select an object and set the thickness of the lines under the "Paint Style" menu.

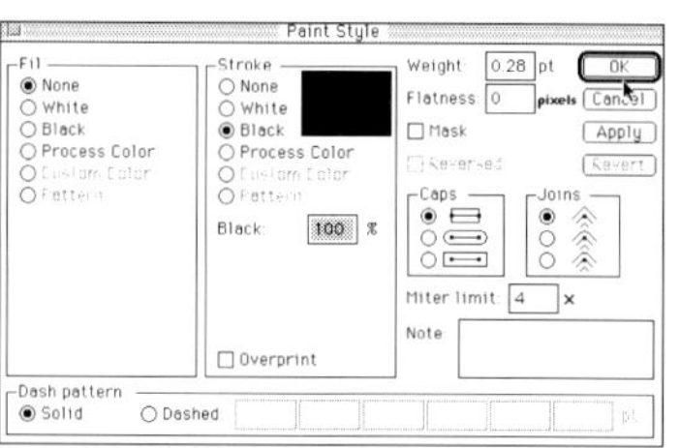

W● ベジェ（Bezier）曲線って、なに？
hat is a Bezier curve?

この名称は、この曲線の考案者であるPierre Bezier氏に由来します。数理計算で作成され、不規則な曲度を描ける曲線のことです。４つの"コントロールポイント"を使って定義されます。ベジェ曲線に複雑な形を描かせたり、曲線の最終ポイントをスムーズにつなぎ合わせることは比較的簡単です。ここでは、ベジェ曲線を使って自由曲線でできる形をつくります。

The line is named after Pierre Bezier. A Bezier line is a curved line based on a mathematical calculation defined along four "control points." With bezier lines you can draw complex forms, and it is fairly easy to smoothly connect the ends of lines. Here is a shape drawn freely with a bezier tool. 3

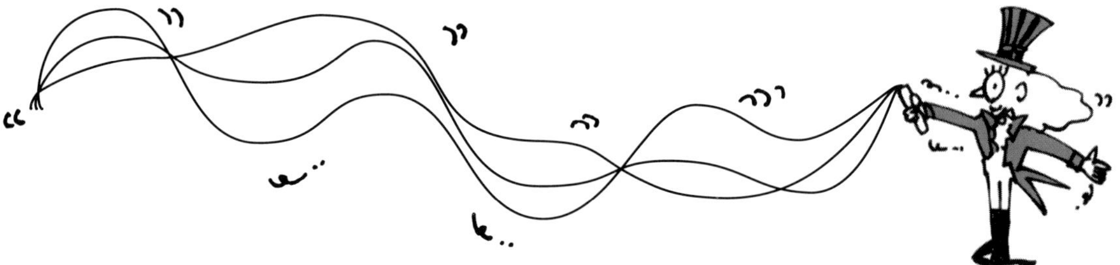

制作プロセス■Production Process

Adobe Illustrator 3.2を使って、曲線を描きます。

※ペンツールは、ドラッグした点から曲線の方向と張りの強さを示す方向線によって曲線を描きます。

Drawing curved lines with Adobe Illustrator 3.2.

Click at starting point and drag. The direction will determine the sharpness and direction of the curve.

1. ペンツールを選び、曲線の始点でマウスボタンを押さえ、曲線を描く方向にドラッグします。次のアンカーポイントでも同様に、曲線を描く方向にドラッグします。

   Select the pen tool, then depress the mouse at the starting point of the line and drag it in the direction you wish to go. Anchor the line to set the curvature, then drag again to the next point.

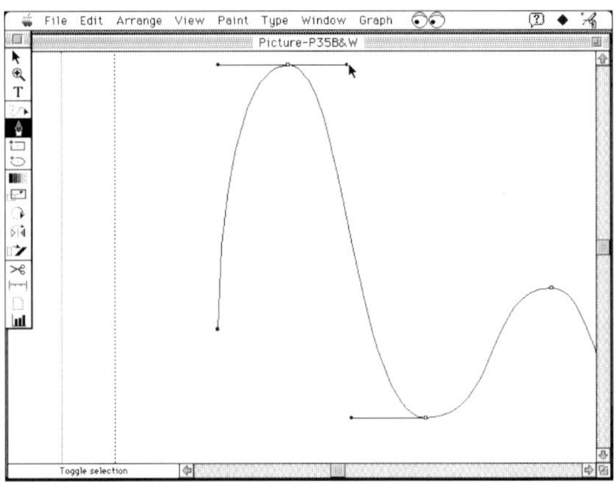

2. 色をつけるオブジェクトを選びます。「ペイント」メニューで線の太さ、図形の色を決めます。ダイアログボックスの「塗りつぶし」「線の設定」で設定します。

   Select an object for coloring. Set the line thickness and object color under the "Paint Style" menu. Dialogue boxes will appear for "Fil" and "Stroke".

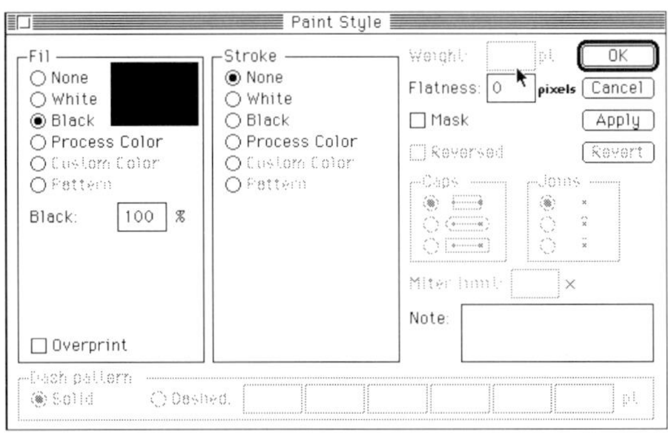

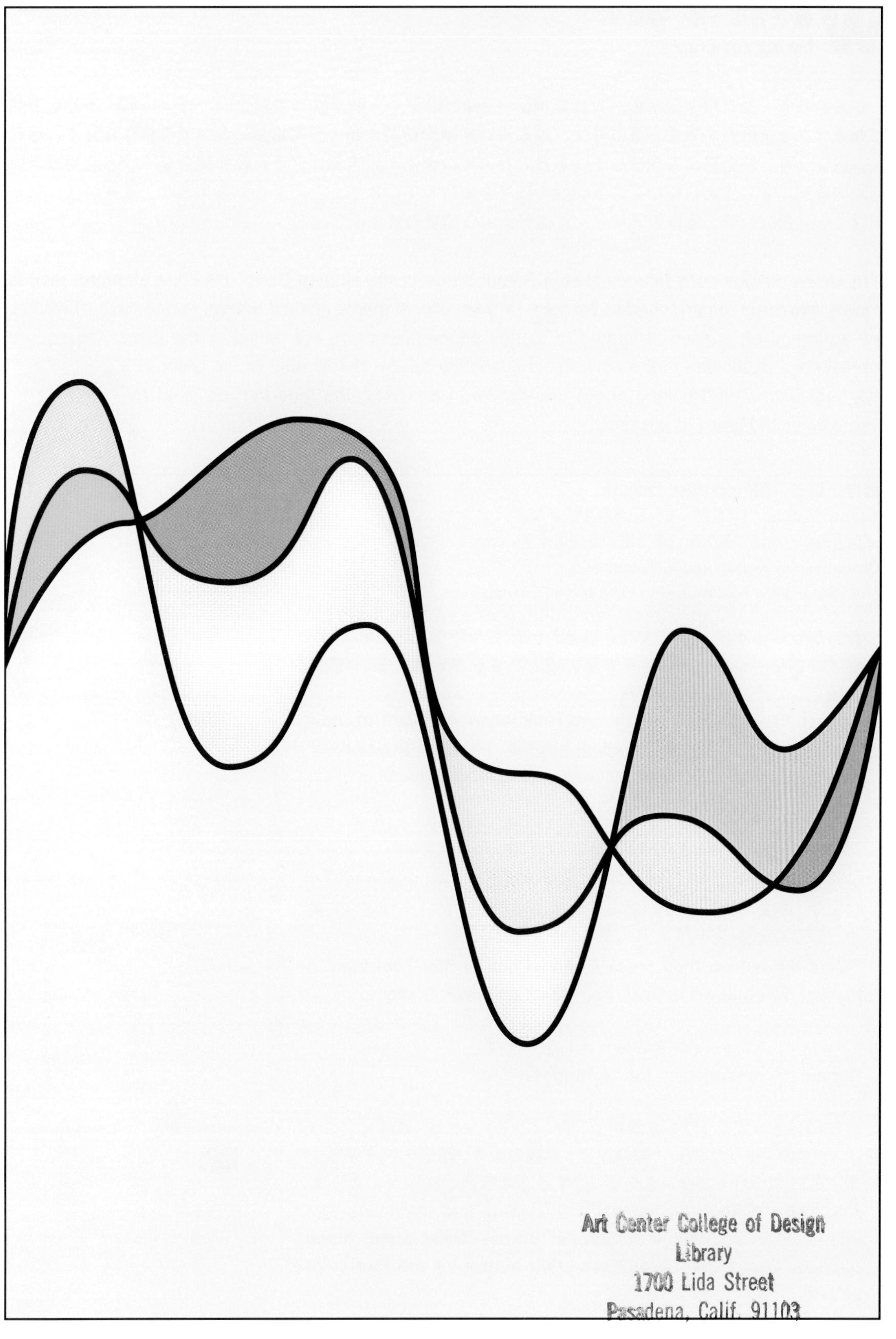

W ● 正方形って、なに？
hat is a square?

レオナルド・ダ・ヴィンチの『人体比例図（1492年）』で人間が立って腕をいっぱいに拡げると正方形になるスケッチは有名です。正方形は、最も古い文字や初期人類の洞窟絵画においても見られます。それは、囲い、家、材の概念を意味しているといわれています。正方形は、それ自体完全な一つの空間概念の極限の集約です。充実した精神の象徴性の秩序を表現しています。このように考えると、正方形は、Macで描くのに用いれば、無限のデザインが拡がるように思われます。

In Leonardo DaVinci's famous sketch "Proportions of the Human Body" (1492), a standing man is shown with arms outstretched in the form of a square. In man's earliest letters, and in cave drawings, the square is often seen. It is said to signify encompassment, the home, or the town. The square represents a distillation of the concept of a singular space, the symbol of the order of a fully-realized spirit. Thinking about the square in this way, the Mac can be used to create unlimited types of designs.

制作プロセス■Production Process
Adobe Illustrator 3.2を使って、正方形を描きます。
※長方形ツールは、長方形（正方形）を描きます。
Drawing squares with Adobe Illustrator 3.2.
The Rectangular Tool is used to draw rectangular squares.

1. 長方形ツールを選び、正方形を描きたいところでクリックします。ダイアログボックスが開き正方形の横と高さを指定します。（数値を設定して正方形を描く方法）
Choose the Rectangular Tool and click when you want to draw the square. A dialogue box will appear. Indicate the desired width and height. (Drawing squares with number values)

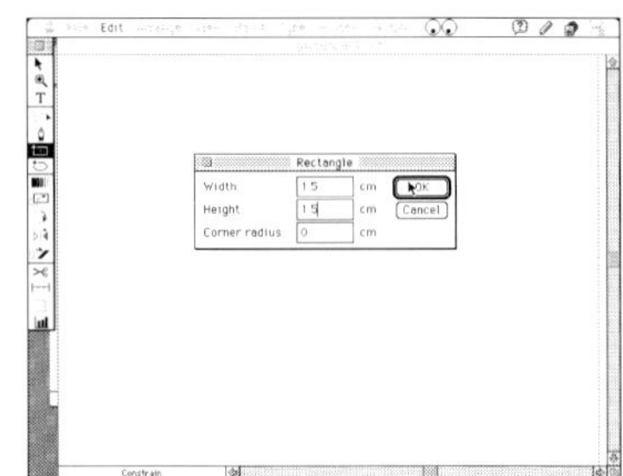

2. オブジェクトを選択し、選択ツールアイコンをOption＋クリックします。移動ダイアログが開き、数値の指定を行ない「コピー」をクリックします。
Select the object, then press Option+Click on the Tool Icon. A moving dialogue will appear. Set values and click "Copy".

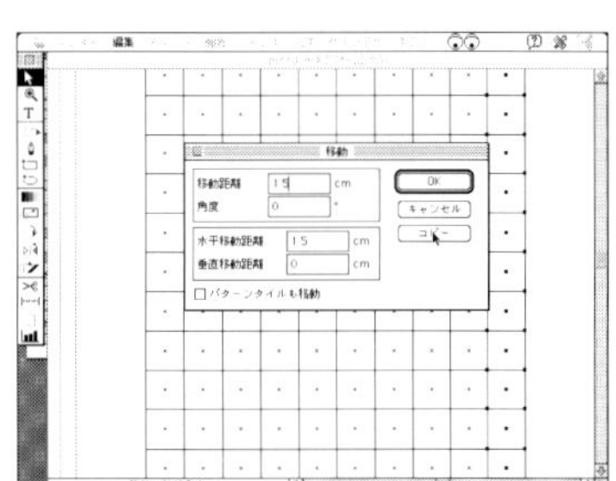

3. 「アレンジ」メニューで作業の繰り返しをします。
Repeat the operation on the "Arrange" menu.

4. 色をつけるオブジェクトを選択し、「ペイント」メニューのダイアログボックスの「塗りつぶし」「線の設定」で線の太さ、図形の色を決めます。プロセスカラーボタンをクリックすると４原色の設定ができます。
Add color. Select the object, then decide line thickness and image color with "Fil" and "Stroke" on the "Paint Style" menu dialogue box. Click the process color button for the four-color setting.

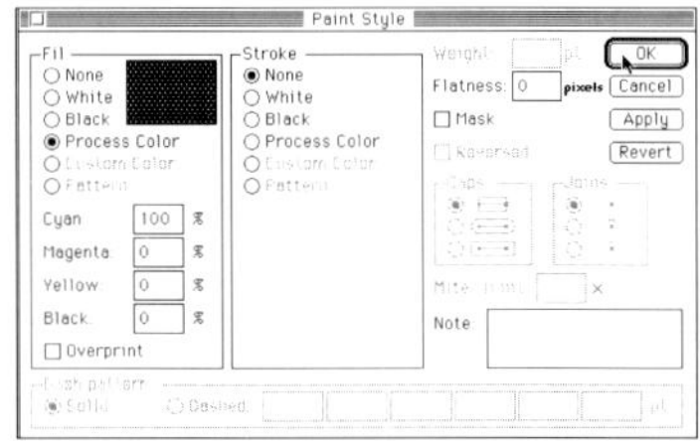

● コンパスを使わないでも円が描けるの？
Can one draw a circle without a compass?

円は昔から、また今日でも、始まりも終わりもない永遠性を示しています。美しい円を描くときにはコンパスをたよりに線を引きますが、なかなか思うようにいきません。ましてや烏口コンパスになるとインクがにじんだりはみ出したりして、もっとうまくいきません。おまけに中心軸の針の穴が大きくあいたりしてがっかりした経験を誰もが持っています。Macを使うといままでのようにコンパスなどの補助的道具を必要とせずに、美しい円を使ったデザインのバリエーションや表現の領域が拡がります。

In ancient times and today, the circle symbolizes that without beginning or end - the eternal. When one draws a circle with a compass it rarely turns out as one wishes. With a beaked compass problems still remain; the ink runs, or the lines fail to meet. Sometimes a large hole is left by the point in the middle of the circle, causing further disappointment. With the Mac, such supplementary tools as the compass are unnecessary. One can draw circles of all kinds, designing an unlimited range of patterns.

制作プロセス■Production Process
Adobe Illustrator 3.2を使って、正円を描きます。
※楕円ツールは、楕円（円）を描きます。
Drawing a circle with Adobe Illustrator 3.2.
The Circle Tool draws circles.

1. 楕円ツールを選び、Shift+Option+ドラッグで円の中心から正円を描きます。(中心から描く方法)
Select the Circle Tool, then use Shift + Option + Drag to draw a circle from center to periphery. (Drawing a circle from the center point)

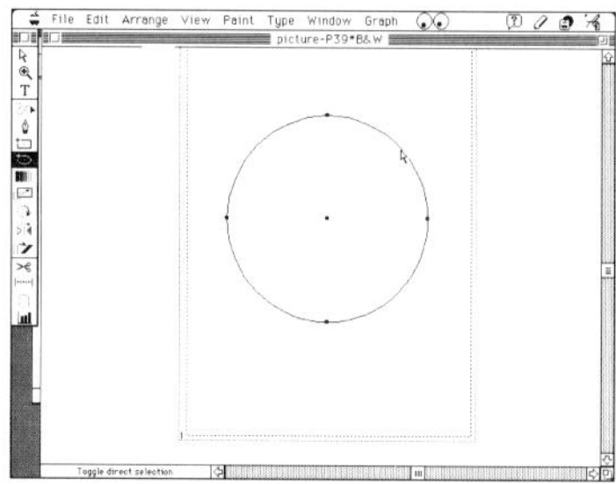

2. オブジェクトを選択します。ツールボックスの拡大・縮小ツールを選択し、Option+クリックします。ダイアログボックスが開き、正確な拡大・縮小、線の太さの数値の指定を行い「コピー」をクリックします。(数値を設定して拡大・縮小をする方法)
Select the object. Select the Scale Tool from the Tool Box, then use Option + Click. A dialogue box will appear, where values for expanding or shrinking can be indicated. Click "Copy". (Expanding or shrinking with number values)

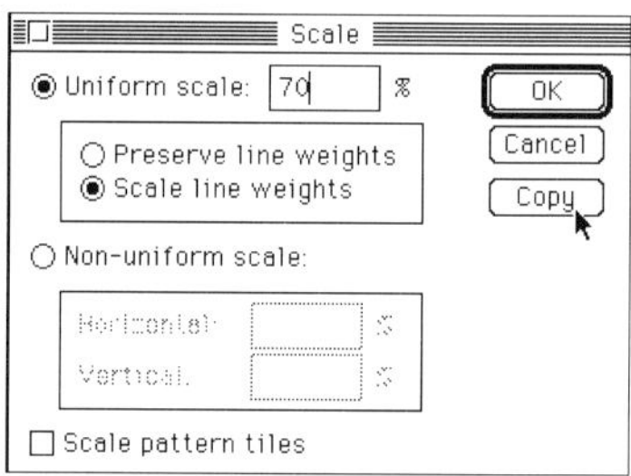

3. 色をつけるオブジェクトを選択します。「ペイント」メニューのダイアログボックスの「塗りつぶし」「線の設定」で線の太さ、図形の色を決めます。プロセスカラーボタンをクリックすると４原色の設定ができます。
Select an object to color. Set "Fil" and "Stroke" in the "Paint Style" menu dialogue box. Click the process color button for the four-color setting.

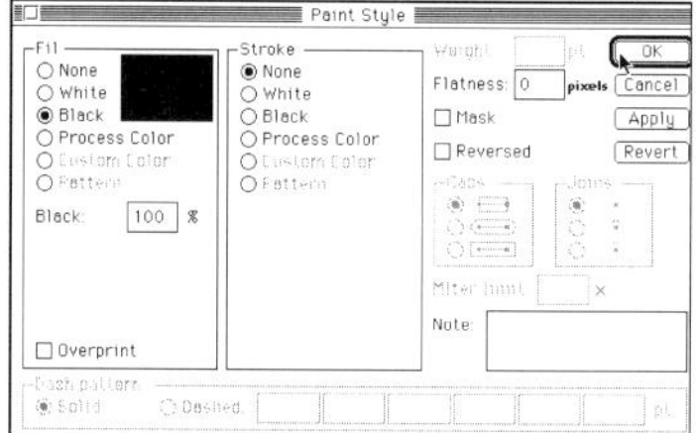

W● 楕円って、なに？
hat is an oval?

楕円を描くのはとても難しくて、グリッド上に座標軸をつくり長軸と単軸の位置を決め、一定の距離になるように点をつなぎあわせて描いたものです。イメージ通りの楕円をつくるのにかなりの時間がかかり、簡単にはいきませんでした。それで、楕円定規にたより、決まり切った楕円の形をよく使いました。ところがMacではマウス操作で思い通りの楕円を使ったデザインと表現が可能になりました。

Drawing an oval is very challenging. One must determine long and short axis points on a grid, then connect them at an even distance. It takes time to do this, and often the result is unsatisfactory. In the past one relied on oval shape guides to draw an oval of predetermined size. But with the Mac, ovals can be drawn freely to create designs of your choice.

■制作プロセス
Adobe Illustrator 3.2を使って、楕円を描きます。
※楕円ツールは、楕円（円）を描きます。
Drawing an oval with Adobe Illustrator 3.2.
Draw an oval with the Oval Tool.

1. 楕円ツールを選び、Option+ドラッグで円の中心から楕円を描きます。（中心から描く方法）
Choose the Oval Tool, then use Option + Drag to draw an oval from center point to periphery. (Drawing an oval from the center point)

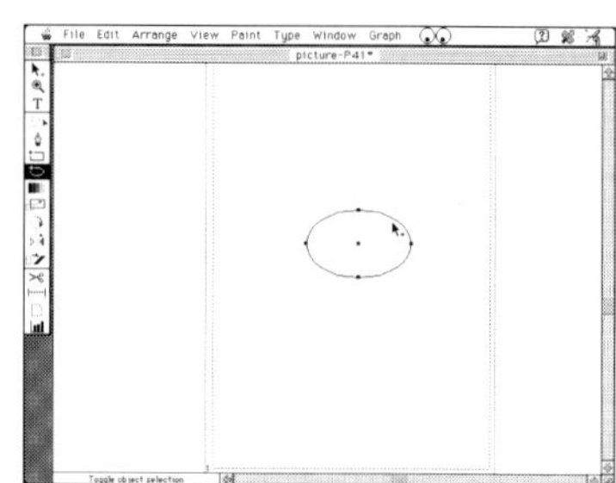

2. オブジェクトを選択します。ツールボックスの拡大・縮小ツールを選択し、Option+クリックします。ダイアログボックスが開き、正確な拡大・縮小（水平方向、垂直方向の拡大・縮小）の数値の指定を行い「コピー」をクリックします。(数値を設定して拡大・縮小をする方法)
Choose the object. Now choose the Scale Tool from the tool box, doing Option+Click. A dialogue box will appear. Indicate values (Horizontal, Vertical) then click "Copy". (Scaling with values)

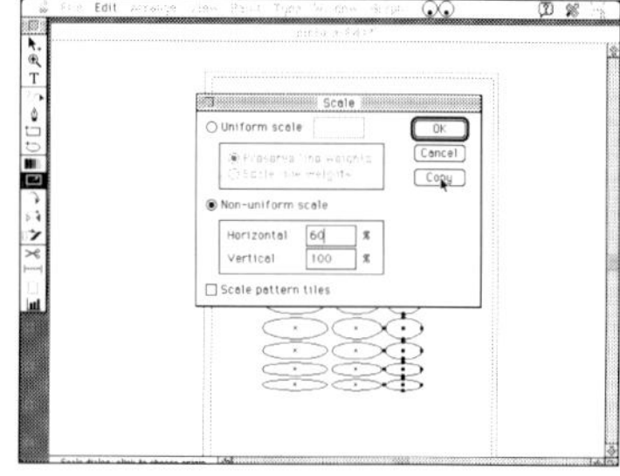

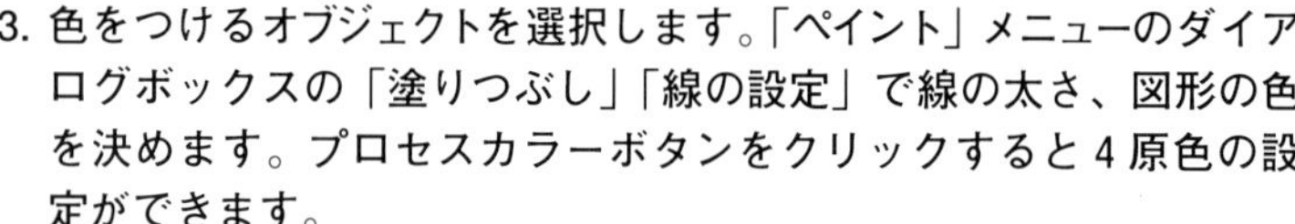

3. 色をつけるオブジェクトを選択します。「ペイント」メニューのダイアログボックスの「塗りつぶし」「線の設定」で線の太さ、図形の色を決めます。プロセスカラーボタンをクリックすると4原色の設定ができます。
Select an object to color. In the "Paint Style" menu dialogue box indicate "Fil" and "Stroke" to determine color and line thickness. Click the process color button for four-color mode.

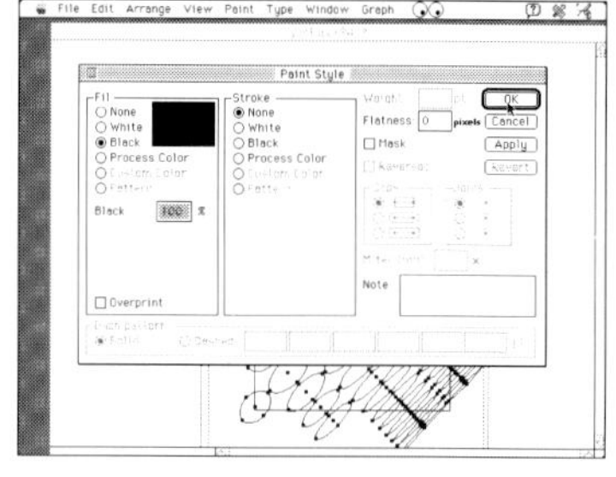

● スキャニングって、なに？
What is scanning?

画像を取り込むことをスキャニングといい、その機器をスキャナといいます。写真や図などの平面原稿をコンピュータで扱うことができるようにデータを変換します。簡単に言えば、気に入った写真や絵などのイメージをコンピュータに取り込む（ことです。

Collecting an image is referred to as "scanning", and the machine which performs this task a "scanner". Two-dimensional images, like photographs and diagrams, can be converted to data by a computer. With a scanner one can easily "read" pictures and photos into a computer.

スキャンモード■Scan Mode

スキャニングのとき扱う原稿によって適したモードで取り込む形式です。それによってイメージをエディット（編集）したり、合成するために最も効果的にスキャニングができます。

When scanning a given work the correct mode must be used. In order to edit and create composite images, the image must be scanned in the right mode.

Line Art

Line Artモードは、トレース図面などのように線や文字によって構成された原稿を取り込むときに使うモードです。白黒の境界線をクッキリときわだたせて取り込むことができます。

The Line Art mode is used when scanning lined diagrams and lettering. This mode produces very sharp black and white lines.

Grayscale

Grayscaleモードは、写真やグラフィックなどの微妙な濃淡を、取り込み表示するためのモードです。原稿の微妙なニュアンスに一番近いイメージで諧調を再現します。

In Gray scale mode the fine shading of photos and graphic images can be captured and reproduced, offering the closest match to the shading and nuance of the original.

Halftone

Halftoneモードは写真や濃淡のあるグラフィックの中間色をスキャニングします。

Halftone mode is effective in catching the intermediate colors of photos and shaded graphic images.

保存フォーマット■Save Format

グラフィックデータの保存には、Paint、PICT、TIFF、EPSFの４タイプのフォーマットがあります。それぞれに合った保存をします。

To save graphic data four types of format are available; Paint, PICT, TIFF and EPSF. These save formats are used for various purposes.

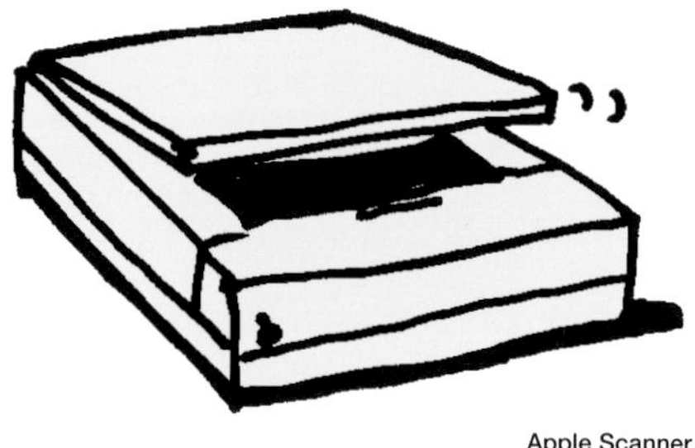

Apple Scanner

U ●出力を上手に使いこなすには？
sing output effectively?

コンピュータには入力と出力があり、出力にもいろいろな機器があります。モニターの中で描くにも、出力のクオリティを想定しなくてはなりません。それは、画像がビットマップでできているからです。PostScriptになったからといって変わるものではありません。デジタル画像の本質です。しかし、これを理解していれば、さまざまな表現にチャレンジできます。そのポイントとは、「どのようなソフトで作ったもの」を「どのように出力したいのか」を明確にすることです。Macのプリンタには、大きく分けてPostScriptプリンタとQuickDrawプリンタがあり、どちらかを選択する必要があります。Macの出力環境は、パーソナルなインクジェットプリンタから、ハイエンドのレーザービームプリンタやイメージセッタまで、目的に応じて幅広い選択が可能になっています。こうした高価な装置を用意してDTP作業のサポートをしてくれるサービスショップを利用するととても便利です。

In computers there is both input and output, and there are various forms of output. When drawing on a computer, one must consider in advance the quality of the output. This is because the image is bit-mapped, a fact which is not altered by postscript. This is the basic quality of graphic images. But once this is understood, various forms of expression can be tried. The point is to consider both the type of soft being used and the type of output available. In Mac printers, there are basically two kinds, Postscript-based and QuickDraw-based, and one must make a choice between these two kinds. With the Mac, one might be printing on anything from an inkjet model to high-end laser printers and image setters, depending upon your objectives. Service shops which offer high-end output equipment to DTP users are very useful and convenient.

プリンタの種類◎Types of Printers

ドット・インパクト方式■Dot-impact method

タイプライターのように、インクリボンをはさんだ印字ヘッド内の針を用紙に打ち付け、インクを転写します。

Works like a typewriter, but using pins (head) instead of type to impact to against ribbon.

サーマル方式■Thermal method

サーマル（熱）を利用して出力する方式の総称であり、種類として、ダイレクト・サーマル方式、熱転写方式、などがあります。

Among methods using thermal printing are Direct Thermal and Thermoelectric.

インク・ジェット方式■Inkjet Method

微細なインク・ノズルを束ねたものをヘッドにして、このノズルからインクを吹きだして紙に定着させる方式です。

The inkjet method employs a bundle of tiny ink nozzles in the head through which ink is blown onto the paper.

OKI MICROLINE 801 PS

W ● MacとCopic（コピック）との融合って、なに？
hat is the fusion of Mac and Copic?

MacとCopicを併用するようになったきっかけは、デジタルとアナログの融合をどのようにしたら、それぞれの持っている特長をいかに活かせるかと考えたことです。その中で特にイラストレーターの立場で描くことをデジタルデザインの中に導入し、新しい表現を模索する必要性を感じました。

Copicの特長は、「1.速乾性である　2.色彩が安定している　3.アルコール性マーカーのためのコピートナーを溶かさない」という点です。さらにこれをMacと融合するためには、プリントアウトした出力用紙そのものにCopicでドローイングします。その後そこにできたものをMacでスキャニングし、操作します。この繰り返しの中でデジタルとアナログの最大な特長を活かしたイラストレーションが生まれました。デジタルとアナログの融合はシステムをつくることと、イラストレーションのデジタルデータ化を進めることによって可能なシミュレーションとバリエーションを拡げます。

The fusion of Mac and Copic was undertaken as a result of efforts to see how the special characteristics of digital and analog might be brought together. Especially in the case of illustration, and digital graphic design, a need was felt for some new form of expression.

The features of Copic are: 1.It is fast; 2.Colors are stable; 3.The copy toner doesn't dissolve alcohol-based marker. Moreover, for the purpose of fusing Copic and Mac, Copic is used for drawing on printout copies. What is completed there is then scanned into a Mac, where it can be manipulated. Through this process the highest capabilities of analog and digital can be achieved. The fusion of analog and digital in a system and the advancement of data digitalization have brought about new possibilities in simulation and variation.

コピック　COPIC

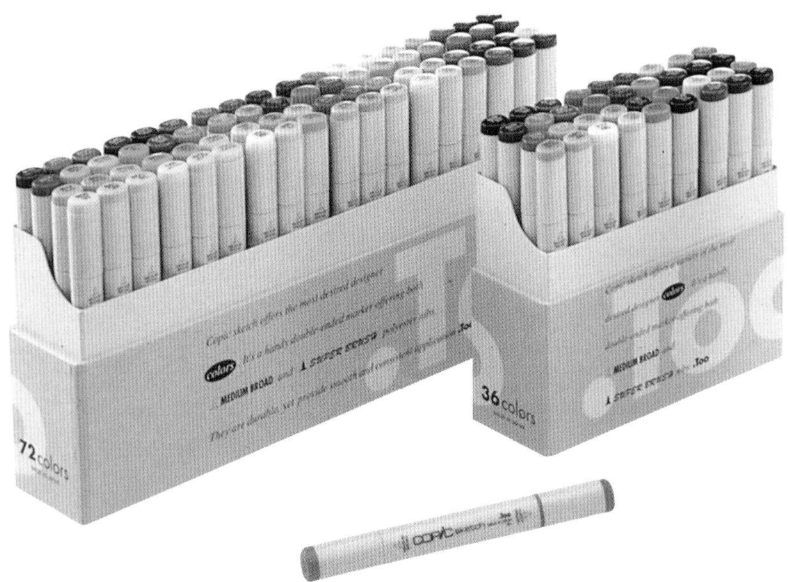

コピックスケッチ　COPIC Sketch

Nude-A

Vegetable

Nude-B

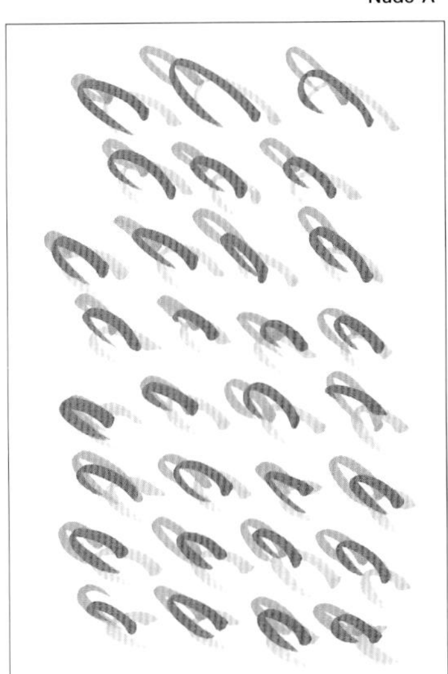

Slip

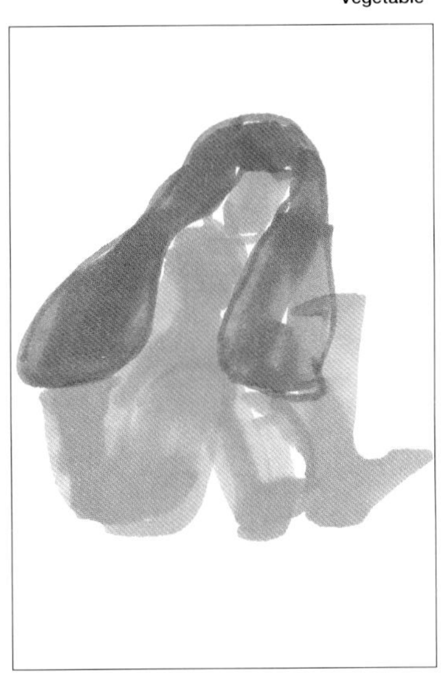

Nude-C

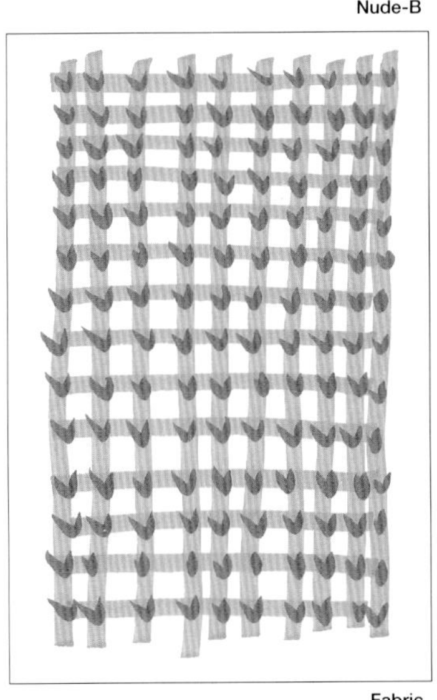

Fabric

Nude-D

Plant

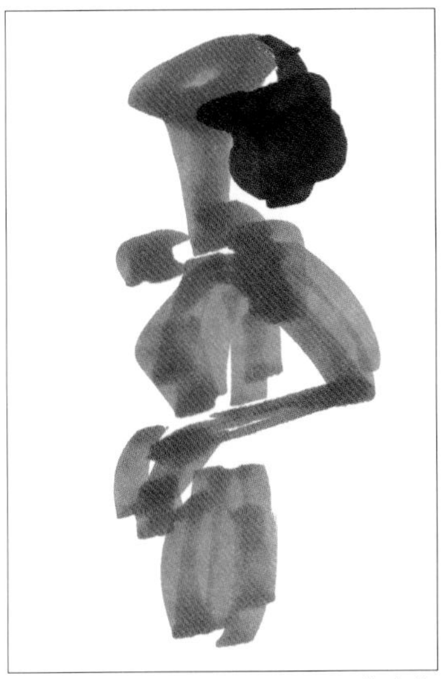

Nude-E

● うさぎを描く
Drawing a rabbit.

現在残っている最古の絵といえば、それは動物画です。約2万年前にスペインや南フランスにある洞窟の天井や壁に当時の人々が描いたものです。野牛、カモシカ、イノシシや野生の馬などを生き生きと巧みに描きました。古代の洞窟絵画は、呪術あるいは宗教的な目的を持って動物を描いたと、一般的に考えられています。水彩ではデューラー（Albrecht Durer 1471-1528）の「野うさぎ（1502年）」の精密な細部表現に驚かされます。

The oldest existing illustrations are of animals. These were drawn by artists on the walls and ceilings of caves in Spain and southern France some twenty thousand years ago. Wild buffalo, antelope, boars and wild horses are brilliantly and clearly drawn in these caves. It is generally thought that these drawings were used for magical or religious purposes. One is impressed by the precise detail of the watercolor "Wild Rabbit" (1502) by Albrecht Durer (1471-1528).

制作プロセス■Production Process *title:* **"うさぎ・Rabbit"**
Adobe Photoshop 2.0のモザイク処理のフィルタを使って描きます。
Drawing with the Mosaic Filter on Adobe Photoshop 2.0.
Original→Scan (GT-6000)→Filter / Stylize-Mosaic→Tool / Paint Bucket→Print out / Color (PIXEL Dio)

◎ Check Point 1. →Scan (GT-6000)
線画イラストをイメージ変換する場合、スキャンするとき、Grayscaleモード（256 Gray）でオリジナルを取り込みます。

To change a lined illustration scan the original sketch in Grayscale Mode (256 Gray).

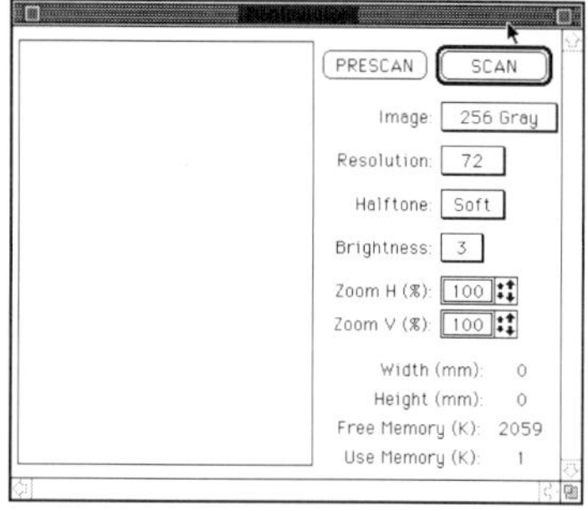

◎ Check Point 2. →Filter / Stylize-Mosaic
モザイク処理のフィルタを使うとき、セルの大きさ（ピクセル平方）によってモザイクタイルの大きさを指定します。

When using the mosaic filter set the Cell Size (pixels square) to determine the size of the mosaic tiles.

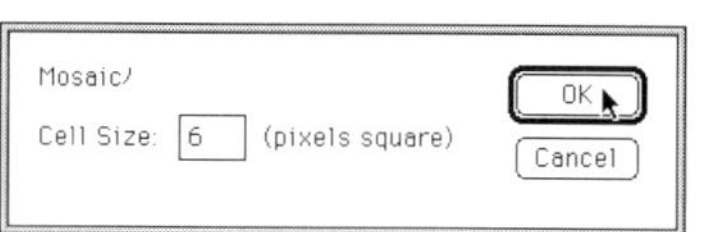

Original

D ● 魚を描く
Drawing a fish.

1853年ロンドン動物園内に世界最初の水族館が生まれました。福沢諭吉はフランスの誇る動植物園ジャルダン・デ・プラントを訪れ、海水魚を入れたガラス水槽を見て大変驚いたそうです。海水魚の泳ぐ姿を横から眺めた初めての体験だったからです。最も一般的な魚の形は、スズキやアジに代表される紡錘形で水中を高速で泳ぐのに適しています。背びれ、胸びれ、腹びれ、尻びれ、尾びれを持ち、体表はうろこにおおわれています。

In 1853, in the London Zoo, the world's first aquarium was built. Yukichi Fukuzawa, who visited France's renowned garden Jardin de Plants, was greatly impressed upon seeing fish in glass tanks. It was the first time he had ever seen fish swimming from the side. The most common fish shapes belong to the spindle-shaped bass and sardine families, which are both fast-swimming fish. They have fins on their backs, bellies and tails, and are covered completely with scales.

制作プロセス■Production Process ***title:* "秋刀魚・Mackerel pike"**
Adobe Photoshop 2.0のエンボスのフィルタを使って描きます。
Drawing with the Mosaic Filter on Adobe Photoshop 2.0.
Original→Paint (COPIC)→Scan (GT-6000)→Edit / Copy, Paste→Filter / Stylize-Emboss→Image / Adjust-Color Balance→Image / Adjust-Hue Saturation→Print out / Color (PIXEL Dio)

◎ Check Point 1. →Paint (COPIC)
コピックでオリジナルのイラストを着色し、スキャンします。

Altering the coloring with Adjust-Color Balance.

◎ Check Point 2. →Image / Adjust-Color Balance
カラーバランスの補正で画像の色味を変更します。

Color is added in Copic, after which the image is scanned.

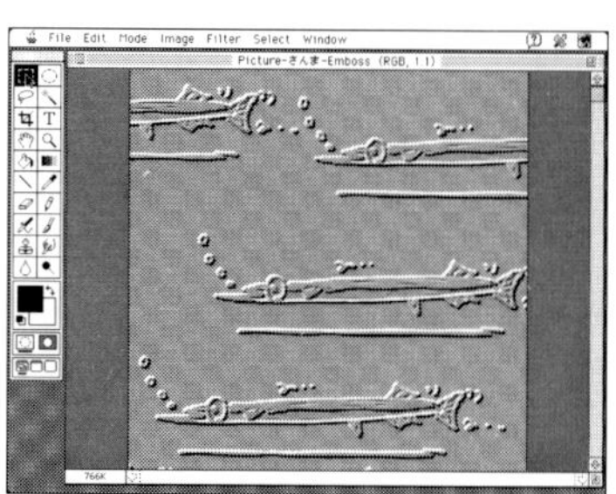

Original→Paint (COPIC)

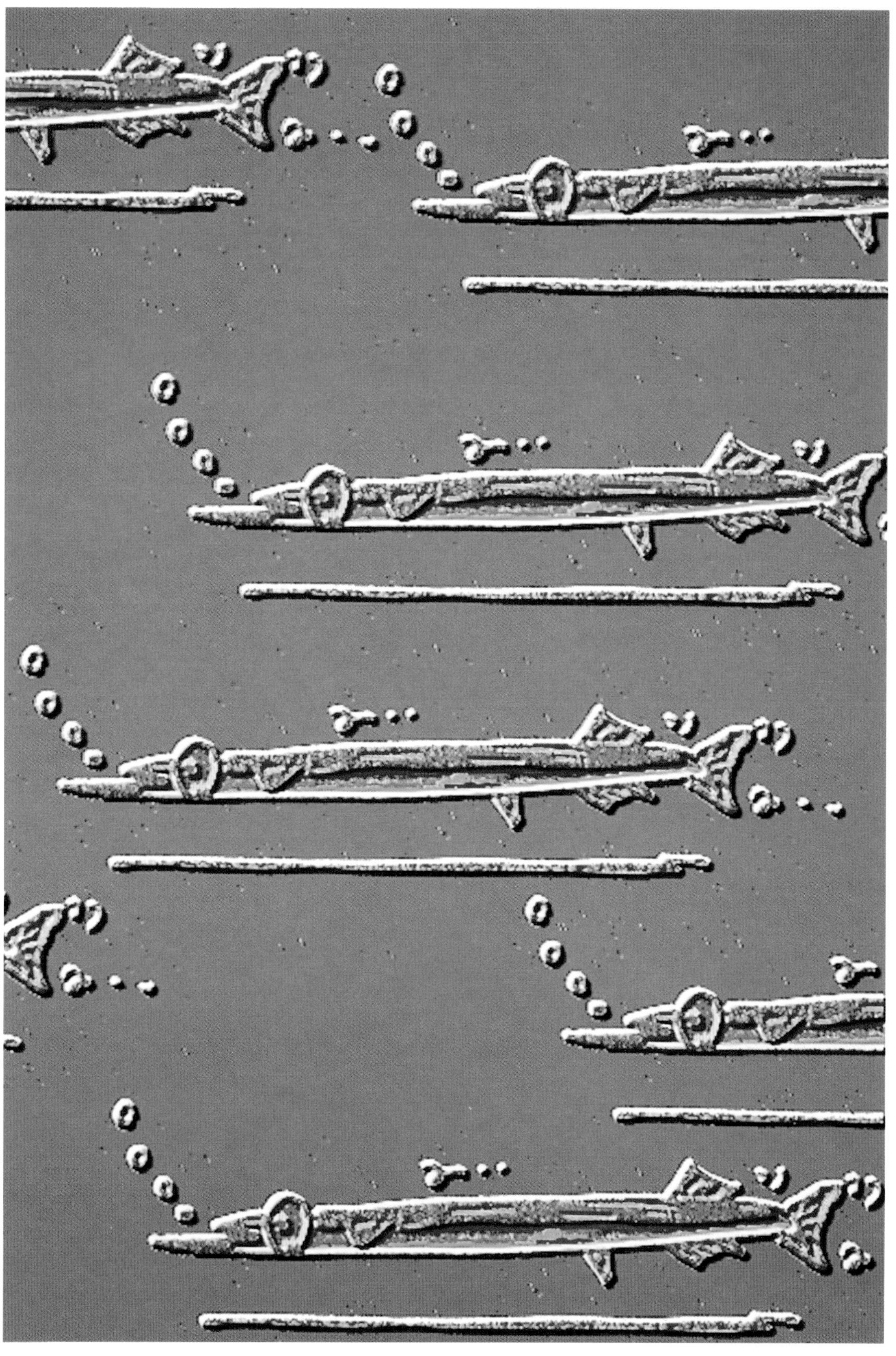

● 鳥を描く Drawing a bird.

鳥類がこの地球上に出現したのは、中生代ジュラ紀にあたります。今からおよそ1憶5千万年前のことです。鳥類の特長は、大空を飛ぶことです。羽毛で作られた翼、軽くて丈夫なからだの構造、鋭い視覚などがあげられます。日本における鳥のスケッチで有名なのは、円山応挙（1733-1795）があげられ、非常に繊細な描写の花鳥画です。バードアートといえば、ジョン・ジェームス・オーデュボン（John James Audubon 1785-1851）とジョン・グールド（John Gould 1804-1881）の鳥類図譜です。

Birds are said to have appeared on earth during the middle of the Jurassic period, about one hundred and fifty million years ago. The forte of birds is their ability to fly in the air. They have wings made of feathers, light but sturdy body structures, and excellent vision. Among the famous sketches or birds by Japanese artists are the very detailed paintings by Oukyo Maruyama (1733-1795). The realistic paintings of John James Audobon (1785-1851) and books by John Gould (1804-1881) are likewise full of fine examples.

制作プロセス■Production Process *title:* **"サギ・Heron"**
Adobe Photoshop 2.0のエンボスのフィルタを使って描きます。
Drawing with the Embossing Filter on Adobe Photoshop 2.0.
Original→Paint (COPIC)→Scan (GT-6000)→Filter / Stylize-Crystallize→Print out / Color (PIXEL Dio)

◎ Check Point 1. →Filter / Stylize-Crystallize

水晶フィルタを使うとき、セルの大きさ（ピクセル平方）によって結晶の大きさを指定し、水晶の結晶のようなテクスチャを画像に与えます。

When using the Crystallize Filter set the Cell Size to determine the size of crystals, giving the image a crystalline appearance.

Crystallize
Cell Size: 10
OK
Cancel

◎ Check Point 2. バリエーション

フィルタには大きく分けてぼかしなどの画像処理系と、変形などの表現技法系があり、画像にさまざまな効果を加えます。

Filters can be divided into two general groups, those which manage shading, and those which alter shape.

Original→Paint (COPIC)

●顔を描く Drawing a face.

人を見るときに最初に目がいくのが顔です。そこには、内面を読み取ることができるほどたくさんの表情を持っています。顔面の筋肉の動きや顔のしわから老若男女の年齢を推測できます。さらに、性格や性質までもが現われ出ることがあります。解剖学的にみれば頭蓋骨から顎のかたちまで人種を超えて美しさを持っているように思われます。レンブラント（Harmensz Rembrant 1606-1669）、ルーベンス（Peter Paul Rubens 1865-1922）やアングル（Jean Auguste Dominique Ingres 1780-1867）などのアカデミックな肖像画からドーミエ（Hanore Victrin Daumier 1808-1879）はじめデフォルメされたカリカチュアまでさまざまな魅力的な作品を目にすることができます。

When looking at a person the first thing we see is the face, where one finds enough expression to read the "inside". From the movement of facial muscles and lines on the face one can determine the ages of men and women. Moreover, personality and temperament can be read in the face. Anatomically speaking, from forehead to jaw the human face seems to possess a transcendent beauty. From the academic portraits of Rembrandt (1606-1669), Rubens (1865-1922), and Ingres (1780-1867), to the deformed caricatures of Daumier (1808-1879) one discovers a variety of bewitching works.

制作プロセス■Production Process ***title:* "ダリと自画像 · Dali and Self-portrait"**
Adobe Illustrator3.2を使って、アウトラインを描きます。
Drawing an outline with Adobe Illustrator 3.2.
Original→Scan (GT-6000)→Tool / Auto Trace→Paint / Style→Edit / Copy, Paste→Print out / Color (PIXEL Dio)

◎ Check Point 1. →Scan (GT-6000)
線画イラストをトレースする場合、スキャンするときLine Artモード（2 Color）でオリジナルを取り込みます。

In order to trace an illustration, scan the original in Line Art Mode (2 color).

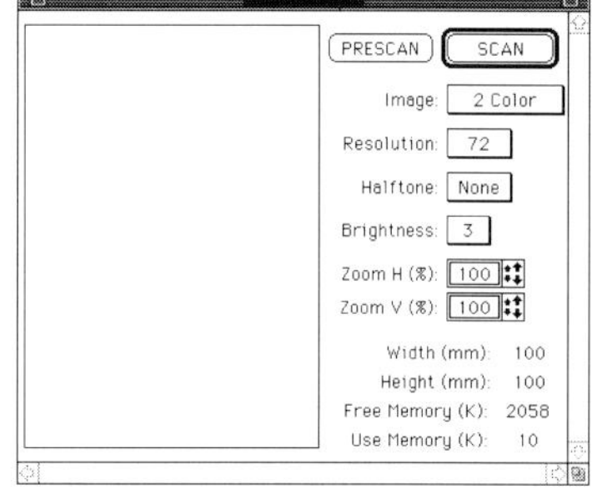

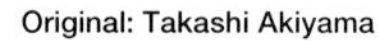
Original: Takashi Akiyama

Original: Dali

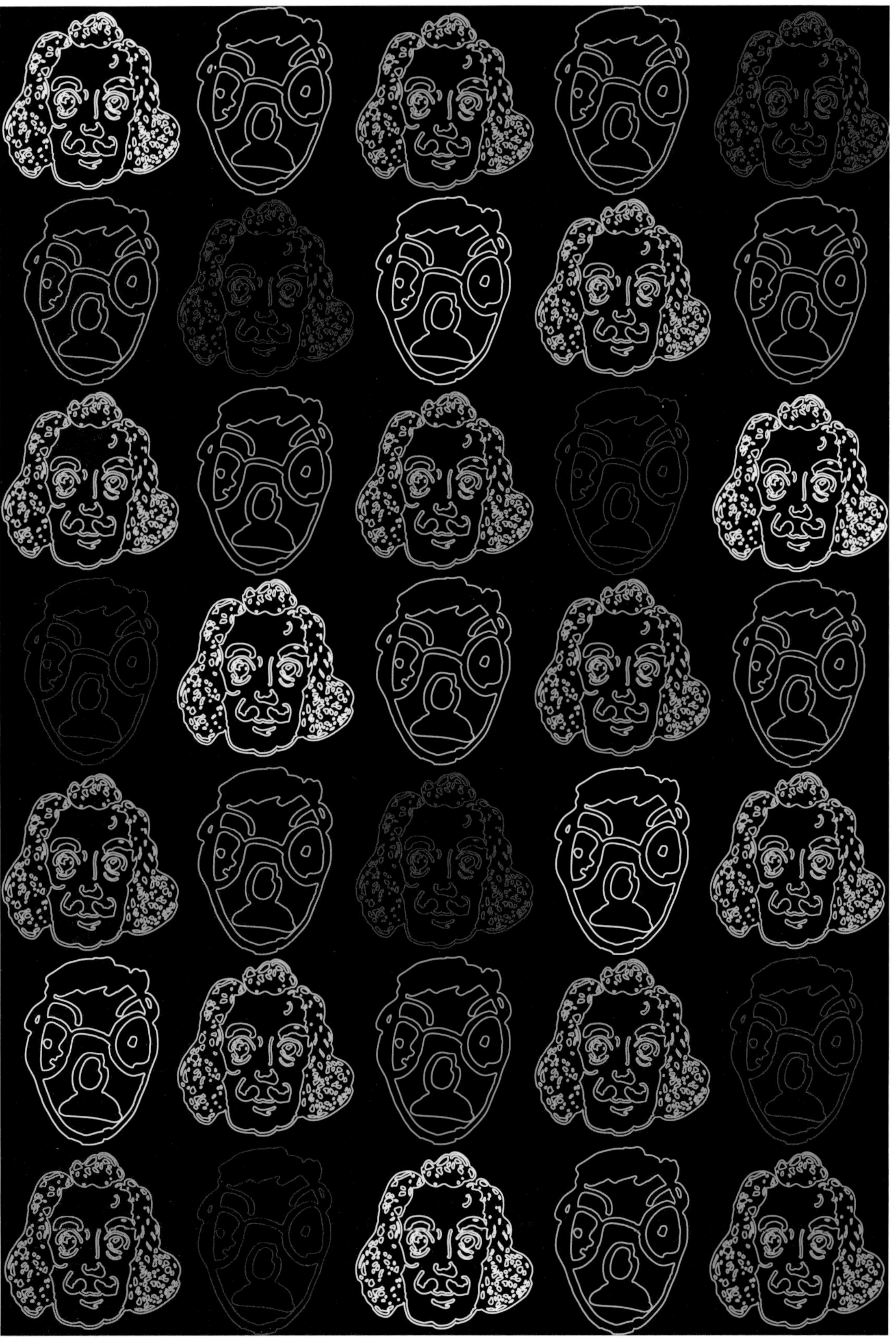

● 人々を描く Drawing people.

群れて生活する動物は、馬、牛や鳥などたくさんいます。人間もその仲間です。ひとりを描くのも大変なのに群衆をまとめて描くのはもっと大変です。しかし、根気よく時間をかけて俯瞰するように描かれたものは、それなりに楽しく鑑賞できるものになります。それは、ひとつひとつの個性ある部分が集合された結果を一望することです。一人一人の性格を描ききるつもりで挑戦してください。

Among the animals which herd or flock are horses, cows, birds and many others. Humans can be included among these. Drawing a single person is difficult, but drawing many together is even more difficult. Nevertheless, by spending plenty of time and working diligently one can create something to be proud of. The pleasure is in the assembly of well-executed individual parts. Concentrate on drawing each person as a distinct individual.

制作プロセス■Production Process *title:* **"人々・People"**
Adobe Photoshop 2.0のぼかしフィルタを使って描きます。
Ilustrating with the Adobe Photoshop 2.0 Blur Filter.
Original→Scan (GT-6000)→Filter / Blur→Tool / Paint Bucket→Print out / Color (PIXEL Dio)

◎ Check Point 1. →Filter / Blur
画像をぼかすフィルタで、何回も繰り返すと強いぼかしがかかります。

Use the Blur Filter over and over for a stronger effect.

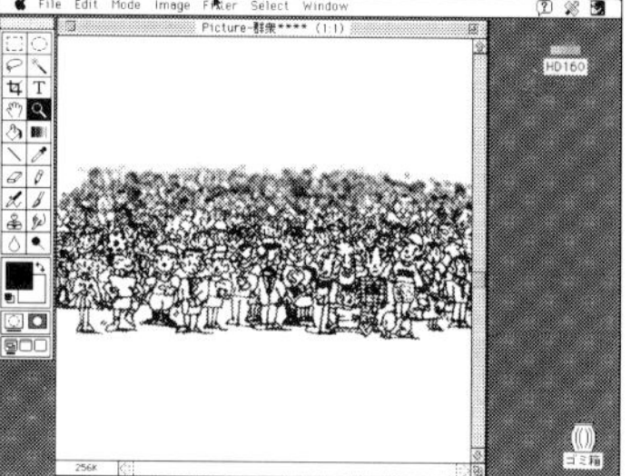

Original

● 植物を描く Drawing plants.

植物は根、茎、葉の栄養器官と、花、果実の生殖器官からできています。自然環境の中で、いろいろな野草がむれて咲く姿はいつの世も私たちのこころに心地好さを感じさせます。鉛筆とスケッチブックを持って野山に出かけ、腰をおろして小さな植物を観察しスケッチをするのは楽しいものです。絵を描くことの醍醐味のひとつです。小さなスケッチブックの中から気に入った絵をスキャニングをし、操作を加え表現の広がりを発見してください。

Plants consist of a nutritive network of roots, stalk and leaves, and a reproductive system made up of flowers and fruit. Everyone has enjoyed the site of a field of blossoming wildflowers. Taking a pencil and sketchbook in hand and going to the mountains to sit before a flower and draw is a great pleasure. This is one of the primary pleasures of painting. You can't take the Mac outside and paint, but you can scan from a sketchbook and discover ways to utilize the input on your Mac.

制作プロセス■Production Process *title:* **"わらび · Bracken"**
Adobe Photoshop 2.0のエフェクトフィルタを使って描きます。
Ilustrating with the Adobe Photoshop 2.0 Effect Filter.
Original→Scan (GT-6000)→Tool / Paint Bucket→Filter / Distort-Zigzagt→Print out / Color (PIXEL Dio)

◎ Check Point 1. →Filter / Distort-Zigzag
波紋のエフェクトフィルタを使うとき、ゆがみの量を大きさ（ピクセル平方）によって指定し、波紋の折り返し数とゆがみ方向を指定します。

When using the Pond Ripples Effect set the Amount of distortion and number of Ridges to determine direction and quantity.

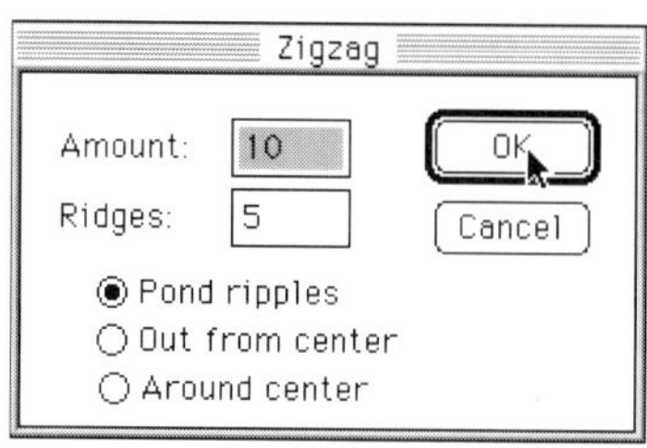

Original

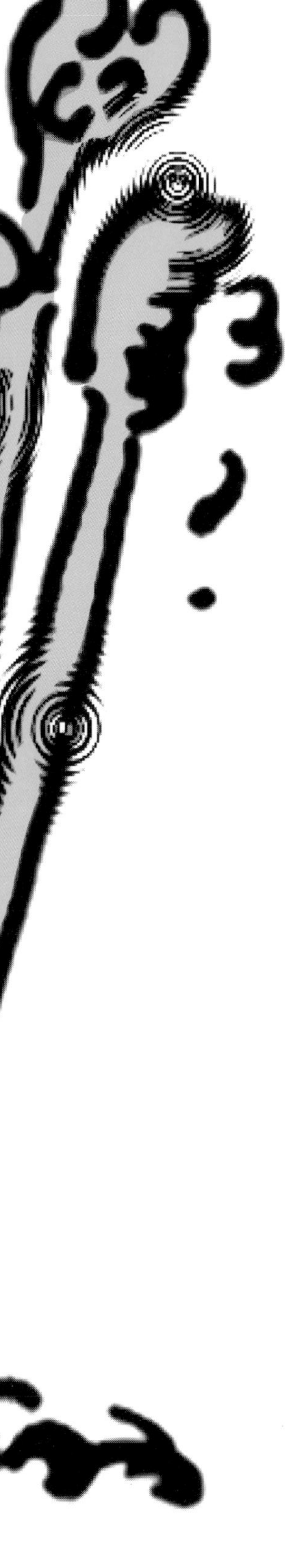

D ●花を描く
Drawing flowers.

一般的に、花を見て気分が悪くなる人はいません。色とりどりの草花たちは楽しく四季の生活空間を演出してくれます。ただし、生き物であることを忘れてはなりません。根は水を吸い、養分をとって生長します。種子をつくり球根を膨らませて子孫を増やします。高等植物の生殖器官が花です。花は、がく、花弁、おしべ、めしべなどの部分からできています。これらはいずれも葉の変形したものです。そのような美しい花を描きたいと私たちは思います。

Generally, there is nobody who can look at a flower and feel bad. Radiantly colored flowers perform throughout the four seasons. But it is important to remember that flowers are living things. The roots absorb water and nutrients. They create seeds and swell bulbs, procreating and increasing in number. The most advanced part of the plant is the flower, its reproductive organ. The flower is composed of the calyx, petals, stamen, pistil and other parts. These are all forms mutated from the leaf. Everyone enjoys drawing beautiful flowers.

制作プロセス■Production Process ***title:* "花・Flowers"**
Adobe Photoshop 2.0の合成コマンドを使って描きます。
Illustrating with a combination of Adobe Photoshop 2.0 commands.
Original→Paint (COPIC)→Scan (GT-6000)→Edit / Copy, Paste→Image / Calculate-Subtract→Print out / Color (PIXEL Dio)

◎ Check Point 1.

2つのチャンネルのピクセルのレベルを計算し、新しい画像を作りだすためのコマンドで、写真でいう多重露光や合成などができます。それぞれの画像サイズ（幅と高さのピクセル数）を同じにし、カラーモードを揃えます。
With a command that calculates pixels on two channels one can create a new image, similar to a double exposure or composite in photography. The image size (height and width in pixels) and color modes must be the same.

◎ Check Point 2. →Image / Calculate-Subtract

Flower 1からFlower 2の画像のレベルを引くことで、現実の写真では不可能な「逆二重露光」をします。
Using the Calculate-Subtract command to reduce the level of Flower 1 by subtracting Flower 2 we can create an impossible "reverse double exposure."

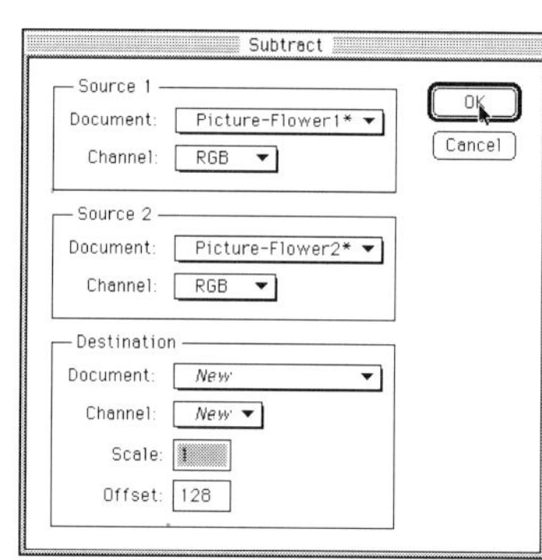

Original: Flower 1

Original: Flower 2

D ● 野菜を描く Drawing vegetables.

四季を大切にする日本人は、食文化の中でも、絵画の中でも野菜は重要な位置をしめています。野菜の季節感を通して四季折々の情緒を楽しみます。特に視覚に訴える野菜の形は、私たちにとって興味あるものです。たとえば、日本工芸の染色、漆芸、陶芸、彫金などの伝統的なデザインの中には、台所から生まれた生活の匂いをモチーフとしたものがたくさんあります。野菜から受ける素朴な味わいもなかなかよいものです。

The Japanese, who pay great respect to the four seasons, make much of the vegetable, whether in cuisine or painting. Through vegetables we experience the pleasures of the four seasons. Vegetables are especially attractive to the eye. In Japanese art, whether it be dyeing, lacquer ware, ceramics, sculpture, or any other traditional form, much of what we see comes from the kitchen. When drawing still lifes, the texture of the vegetable is particularly stimulating to our senses.

制作プロセス■Production Process *title:* **"だいこん · Radish"**
Adobe Photoshop2.0の発光エフェクトを使って描きます。
Illustrating with the Adobe Phtoshop 2.0 Colors Effect.
Original, Photo→Scan (GT-6000)→Tool / Magic Wand→Select / Inverse→Edit / Copy→Select / Similar→Window / Show color→Edit / Stroke→Edit / Copy, Paste→Edit / Composite Controls→Print out / Color (PIXEL Dio)

◎ Check Point 1. →Window / Show color
画像が発光しているようにするエフェクトです。発光させる色は、彩度が高く、明るい色が効果的です。

An effect which makes the object appear to give off light. Brilliant colors are most effective in producing light.

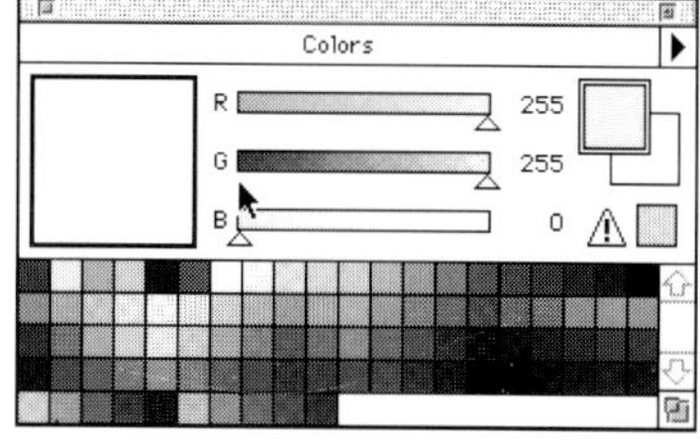

◎ Check Point 2. →Edit / Stroke
境界線を描くとき、幅、不透明度、位置を指定します。何回も繰り返すことによって発光を強くします。

When drawing the border, set the width, opacity and positioning. By repeating the command several times the radiance will be increased.

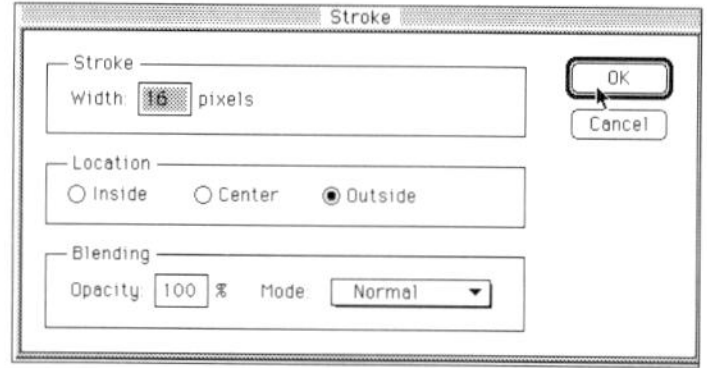

Photo

Original

D● 静物を描く
Drawing still lifes.

モランディ（Giorgio Morandi 1890-1964）の静かな深みのある静物画は、なぜ強く心に響くのでしょう。それは激しいドラマティックな表現とは異なり、抽象的な形体を中心とした静謐な静物空間をつくりあげているからです。またシャルダン（Jean Baptiste Simeon Chardin 1699-1779）の正直でつつましく、日常を静かな目で凝視した静物画やピカソ（Pablo Picasso 1881-1973）やブラック（Georges Braque 1882-1963）のキュビズムの静物画などを見ても、静物を描くことの魅力は、限りない創造力をかきたてます。

Why do the quiet, searching still lifes of Giorgio Morandi (1890-1964) attract us so? Unlike highly dramatic works, these still lifes are constructed around a central abstract form, creating of space of undisturbed tranquillity. One can also look at the direct but understated resolutions in the still lifes of Jean Baptiste Simeon Chardin (1699-1779), or at the still lifes of the cubists Pablo Picasso (1881-1973) and Georges Braque (1882-1963) and see the same charm, which is brought forth by unlimited creative power.

制作プロセス■Production Process *title:* **"ビン · Bottle"**
Adobe Photoshop 2.0のエフェクトフィルタを使って描きます。
Illustrating with Adobe Photoshop 2.0 Effect Filters.
Original→Scan (GT-6000)→Mode /RGB color→Filter / Stylize-Find Edges→Filter / Stylize-Trace Contour→Print out / Color (PIXEL Dio)

◎ Check Point 1. →Filter / Stylize-Find Edges
画像の輪郭部分をその色のレベルの変化の度合いにしたがって描き出す輪郭検出フィルタです。

With the Stylize-Find Edges Filter you can trace the silhouette based on the mixture of coloring in the outline.

◎ Check Point 2. →Mode/RGB color→Filter/Stylize-Trace Contour
RGBカラーとCMYKカラーでは効果が異なり、色のレベルの変化が激しいところほど強く表示されます。

RGB and CMYK coloring achieve different effects, which become more obvious as color variation increases.

Original

● 風景を描く Drawing scenery.

「自然こそすべての始まりである」と、コロー（Jean Baptiste Camille Corot 1796-1875）は言い、写生の正確さと光の拡散によって、空気を微妙な色彩表現でとらえました。いっぽうタナー（Joseph Mallamallord William Turner 1775-1851）は、このうえない速さで自然が織りなすドラマを描きました。日本では、長谷川等伯（1539-1610）の「松林図屏風」の前に立つと、私たちの美しい風土を思い、豊かな詩情に共感を覚えます。幕末の浮世絵師、歌川広重（1797-1858）は、雨や雪の情景を好んでとりあげ、すぐれた風景版画をつくりました。

According to Jean Baptiste Camille Corot (1796-1875) "everything begins with nature," and he reproduced the objects and lighting of his scenes with extraordinary accuracy. On the other hand, Joseph Mallamallord William Turner (1775-1851) captured the dramatic weave of nature in its unfathomable distance. Standing in front of "A Pine Forest," by Hasegawa Touhaku Hasegawa (1539-1610), we see beautiful scenery and at the same time receive a full sense of the poetic. Hirosige Utagawa (1797-1858) the ukiyoe master of the late Edo period, was fond of rain and snow, and cut many beautiful woodblock scenes.

制作プロセス■Production Process *title:* **"海岸の風景・View of Seashore"**
Adobe Photoshop2.0のエフェクトフィルタを使って描きます。
Illustrating with Adobe Photoshop 2.0 Effect Filters.
Original→Scan (GT-6000)→Mode / RGB color→Image / Map-Posterize→Filter / Stylize-Scatter Horizontal→Image / Adjust-Brightness, Contrast→Filter / Sharpen→Filter / Other-Minimum→Print out / Color (PIXEL Dio)

◎ Check Point 1. →Image / Adjust-Brightness, Contrast
画像全体の明るさとコントラストのレベルを調節します。画像のハイライトを飛ばしたり、シャドウをつぶしたりして効果を出します。

Adjust the overall brightness and contrast levels of the image. Achieve effects by highlighting or adding shadow.

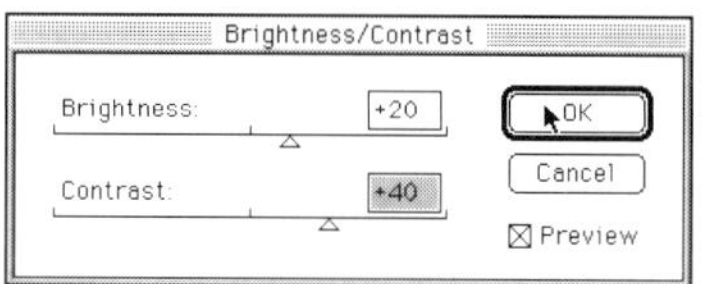

◎ Check Point 2. →Filter / Other-Minimum
数値で指定したピクセル平方の範囲内で一番暗いピクセルのレベルに合わせるフィルタです。

This filter adjusts to the level of the darkest pixels in the specified area.

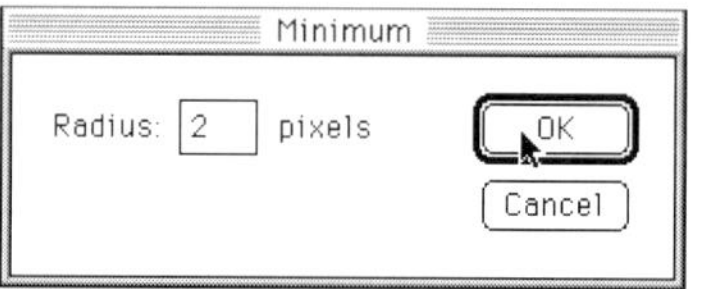

Original

D ●抽象を描く
Drawing the abstract.

20世紀に入ってから幾何学的な形象をよりどころにして、抽象画が生まれます。モンドリアン（Pieter Cornelis Mondriaan 1872-1944）は、写実的な「木」の表現を徐々に単純化しながら、最終的には幾何学的な秩序が生まれました。カンディンスキー（Wassily Kandinsky 1866-1944）は、点、線、面の集積に還元される独立した造形を行ないました。絵の具の「にじみ」などの偶然によって生まれる形や線などを用いた表現をアンフォルメルと言います。このように形や色は、秩序とリズムを生み、それぞれ感情や意味を感じさせることがあります。

Beginning in the twentieth century art began to depart from geometric images to abstract paintings. Pieter Cornelis Mondriaan (1872-1944) began with the tree, but gradually simplified and ordered its form based on geometric principles. Wassily Kandinsky (1866-1944) used points, lines and surfaces to evolve extremely unique forms. The forms that are created coincidentally by the ooze of the tools of painting might be referred to as the "unformal." Here form and color achieve their own rhythm, and make us feel various emotions and meanings.

制作プロセス■Production Process *title:* "**抽象**・Abstraction"
Adobe Photoshop 2.5のエフェクトフィルタを使って描きます。
Illustrating with Adobe Photoshop 2.5 Effect Filters.
Original→Scan (GT-6000)→Edit / Copy, Paste→Edit / Composite Controls→Filter / Stylize-Fragment→Image / Adjust-Hue, Saturation→Image / Effects-Scale→Image / Adjust-Color Balance→Tool / Cropping→Filter / Watercolor→Print out / Color (PIXEL Dio)

◎ Check Point 1. →Edit / Composite Controls
ペーストした選択範囲内の画像とその下にある画像との関係を調節し、選択範囲内の画像を半透明にしたりすることができます。

The relationship between the pasted element and the area below it is adjusted. The image in the selected area can be made semi-transparent, etc.

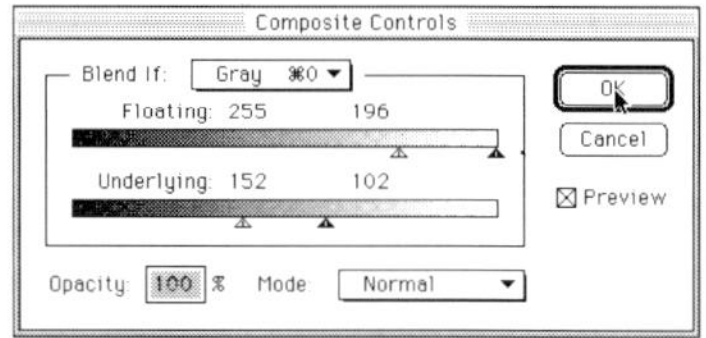

◎ Check Point 2. →Filter / Watercolor
水彩絵の具で描いたような絵画作品に仕上げることができるフィルタです。

This filter allows one to make an image appear like a watercolor painting.

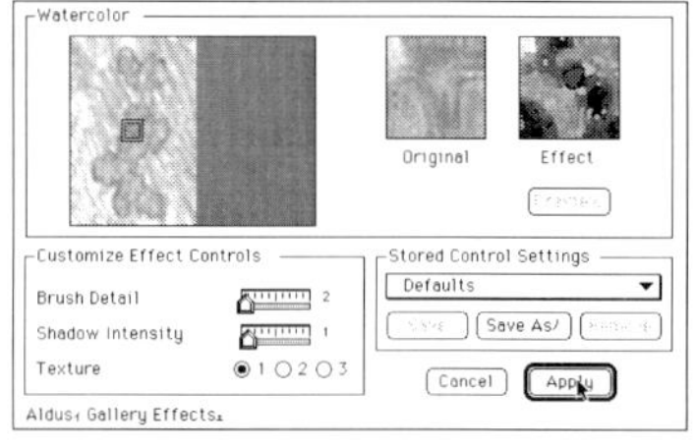

Original　Original

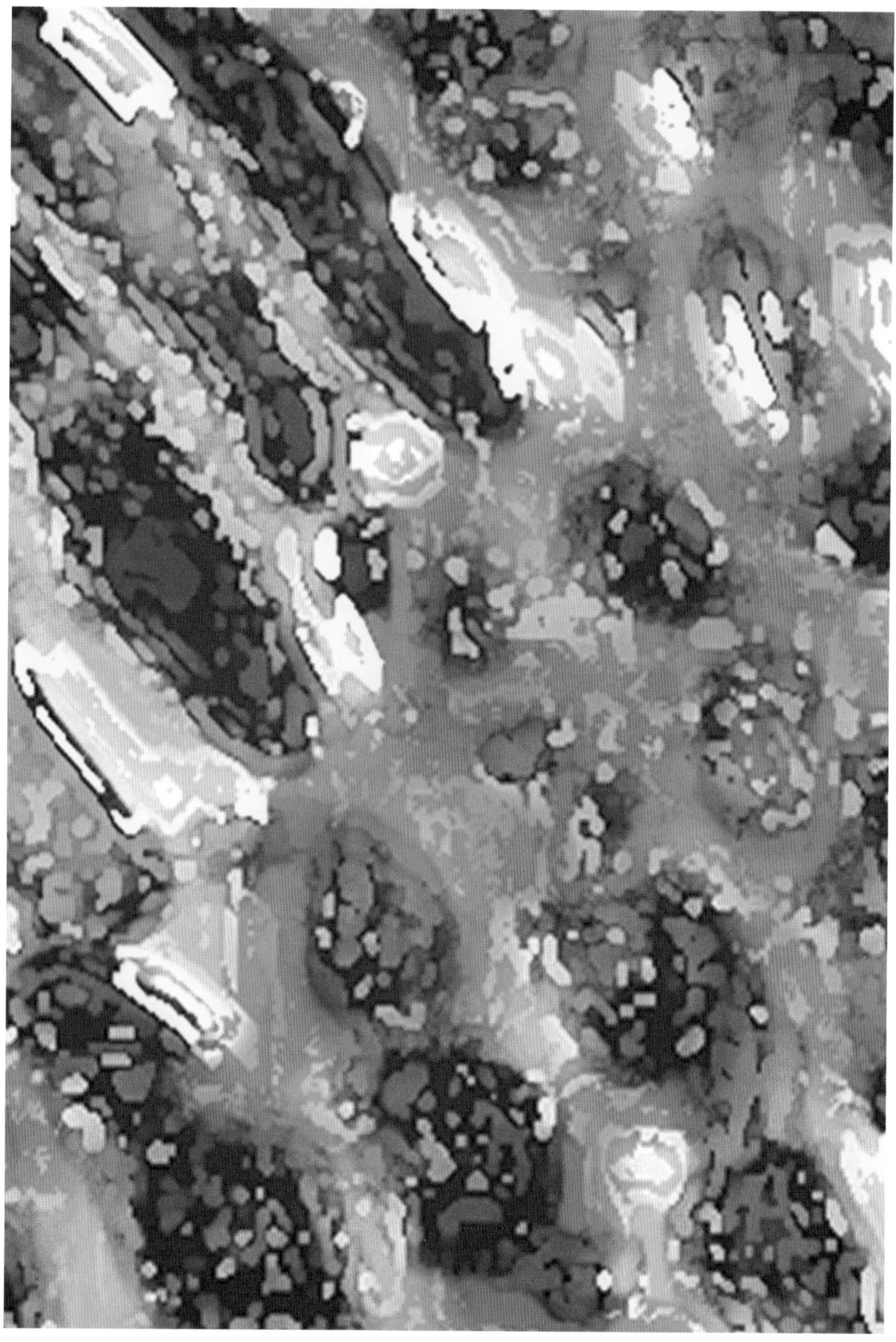

Chapter

W●ステコン技法の家系図って、なに？
What is the family tree of the Stacom method?

「デジタルとアナログはどう違うの？」（p.11）の中で、この本では、「手で描くことをアナログ、Macで描くことをデジタル」と位置づけました。「アナログとデジタルの融合って、なに？」（p.18）の中では「それぞれの持っている特徴を分析し、いかに活かすかを考えました。特にイラストレーターの立場で描くことをデジタルデザインの中に導入しました」と述べました。これらのことから発想したのがステコン技法の家系図です。

デジタルデザインの考え方の基本は、家系図のようなつながりと広がりがあるように思われます。アナログの描くということと組み合わせ、デジタルとアナログの融合から生まれた新たな家系図を作りました。それはインプットとアウトプットを繰り返しながら、非常に単純な操作によって、しかもデジタルとアナログを活かしたシステムです。最大の特徴は、プリントアウトした紙にコピックで色と図柄を描き加え、スキャンするという手法です。それはイラストレーターにとってデジタルと付き合うのに非常に理解しやすい手法です。

In "What is the difference between digital and analog?" (p.11) we stipulated that drawing by hand was analog, while drawing on the Mac was digital. In "What is meant by the fusion of analog and digital?" (p.18) we said: "Various capabilities of the computer can be analyzed, and ways to utilize them thought of. Especially from the standpoint of the illustrator, these capabilities can be introduced into digital design." These ideas can be included in the Stacom method family.

The basic concepts of digital design are connected and spread out like a family tree. Using analog drawing, digital and analog have been combined to create a new family tree of techniques. By repeating input and output, and utilizing other very simple methods, the system makes full use of digital and analog. The greatest single strength of the system is the ability to print out, make additions in copic, and then scan again into the system. This is one very simple way for the illustrator to utilize the computer.

W ●ステコン技法の色の特徴は？
hat is the color feature of the Stacom method?

Macの色彩は、絵の具の混色（減法混色）とは異なり光の３原色の赤(R) 緑(G) 青(B) の加法混色で決定します。これをRGB（Red Green Blue）と呼びます。色数は各色の輝度のレベルの段階によります。RGBそれぞれに、256諧調が割り当てられているため、３色の組み合わせは256の３乗、約1677万色の色彩表現が可能となります。また、RGBはカラーモニターに画像を送る際の信号（RGB signal）にも使用されています。つまり、ステコン技法の発色は、アナログの色とは違いデジタル特有の輝きを持っています。ここに添付してあるフロッピーディスクの画像データは、リアルタイムに読者に再現されます。

On a Mac, unlike colors drawn with other tools, one must mix the basic colors of red, green and blue. These are often referred to simply as RGB. The number of colors under each category depends on the level of brilliance. But within each of the colors of the RGB spectrum are 256 color divisions; each of these three colors can be further raised or lowered in brilliance to create a possibility of more than 16,000,000,000 colors. The color monitor's image is created with a signal, known as the RGB signal. What makes digital coloring different from analog coloring is the color brilliance. And anyone can reproduce the brilliant color of the Stacom method directly from a floppy disk, in real time.

Face A-2

ステコン技法の家系図の考え方で、顔をモチーフにインプットとアウトプットを繰り返しながら制作します。ここでは、オリジナル（ペンで描いたもの）をスキャニングし、制作プロセスにあるように操作します。それをモノクロでプリントアウトしたものが下の家系図の“A-1”と“B-1”です。さらに“A-1”にコピックで描き加え、表現していきます。(次ページへつづく)

Using faces as a motif, a family tree of the Stacom method is created. The faces were input and output repeatedly. The original was drawn with a pen and scanned, and then manipulated as shown in the process. The monochrome print-out of the "A-1" and "B-1" family tree is shown below. Additional expression is added to the "A-1" face in copic. (See following page.)

制作プロセス■Production Process
Adobe Photoshop 2.0のを使って描きます。
Illustrating with Adobe Photoshop 2.0.
Original→Scan (GT-6000)→Edit / Stroke→Print out / Monochrome (MICROLINE 801PS)→Paint (COPIC)

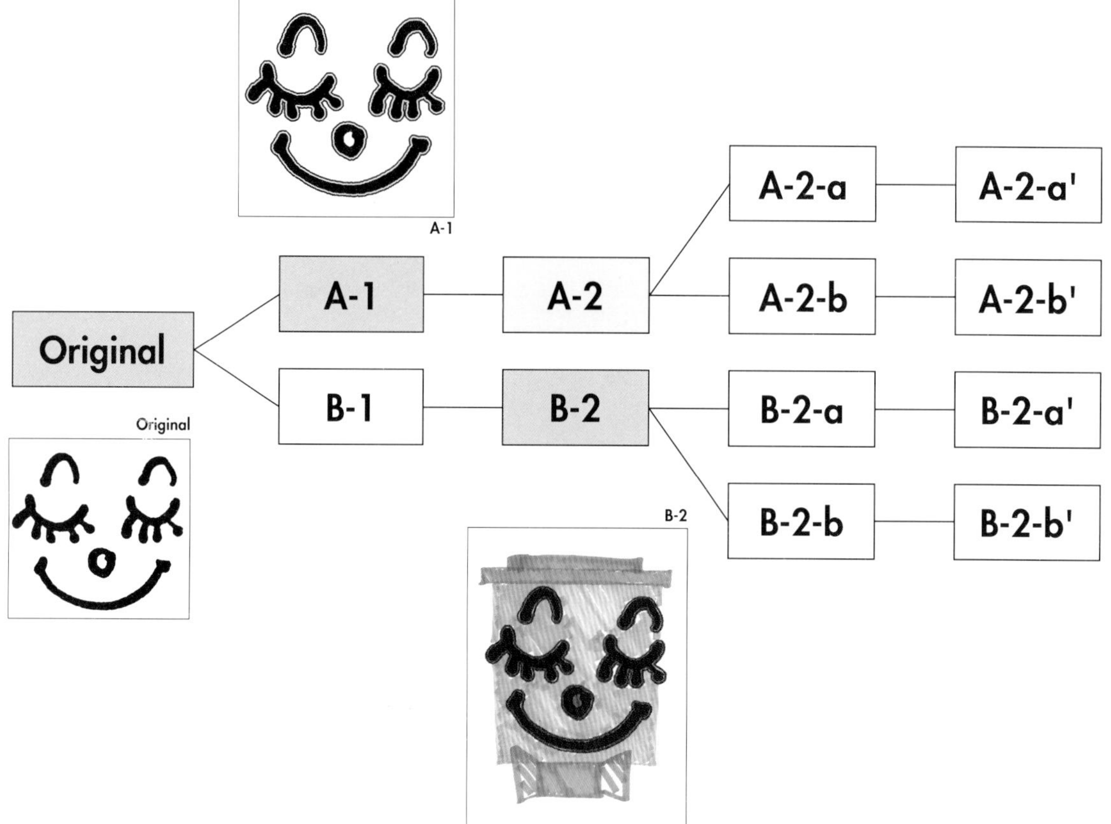

Face B-2-b

前ページでできた“A- 2”と同じ階層にある“B- 2”も、“A- 2”と同じようにプリントアウトされたものにコピックで表現し、新たなバリエーションの顔を描きます。そしてそのイラストレーションをスキャニングし、操作を加え“B- 2 -a”と“B- 2 -b”ができました。同じように“A- 2”に操作を加え“A- 2 -a”と“A- 2 -b”が生まれ、さらに“A- 2 -a'”と“A- 2 -b'”へとデジタル表現は無限の広がりを見せます。

In the same way as "A-2", the "B-2" face at the same stage as "A-2" is printed and filled in with copic. Then the illustration is scanned and manipulated to create "A-2-a" and "A-2-b". In the same way "A-2-a'" and "A-2-b'" are created, displaying the unlimited expressive power of digital.

制作プロセス■Production Process
Original→Scan (GT-6000)→Edit / Stroke→Print out / Monochrome (MICROLINE 801PS)→Paint (COPIC)→Scan (GT-6000)→Filter / Stylize-Emboss→Print out / Color (PIXEL Dio)

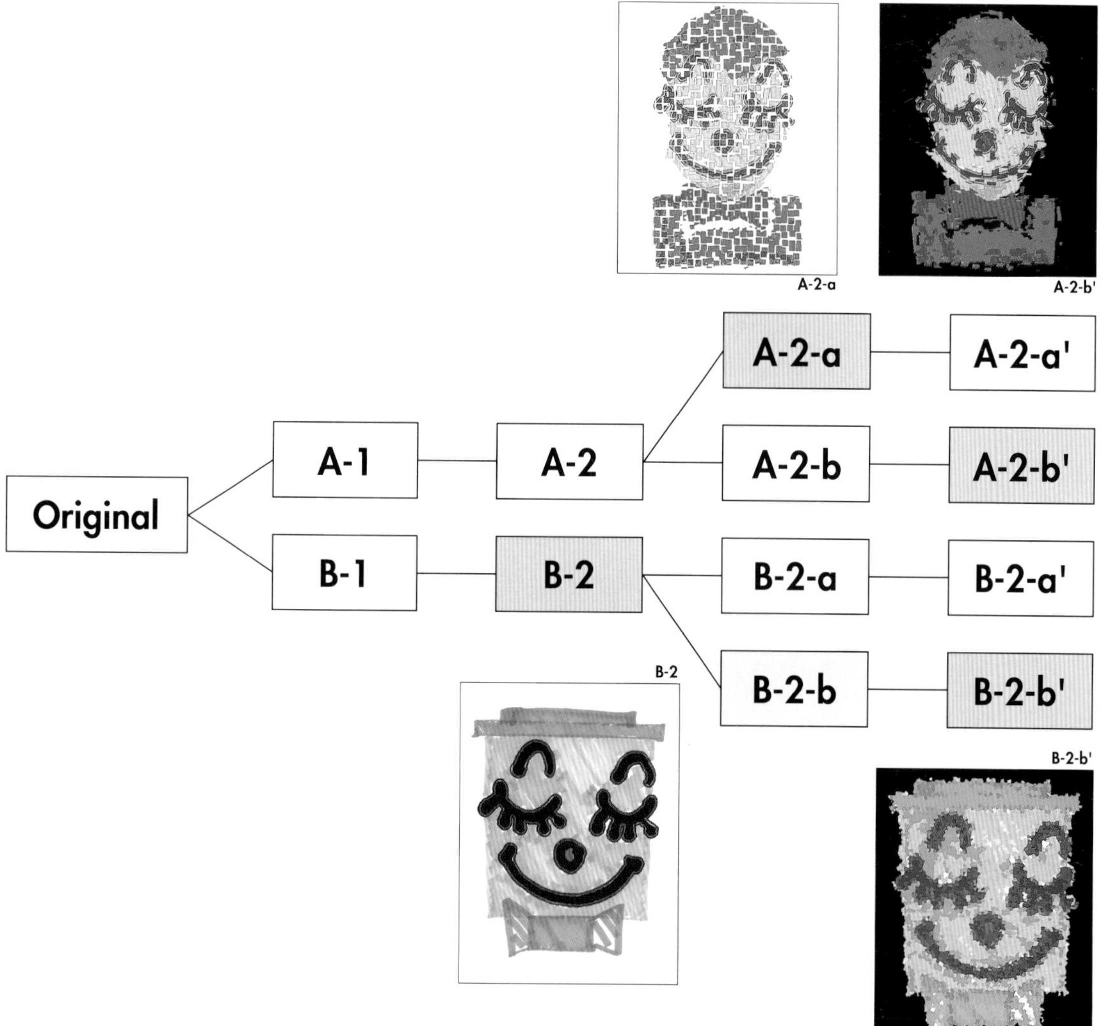

Nude A-2

Faceの家系図よりも複雑になった実例Nudeを展開します。まず、コピックで女性のヌードスケッチをします。コピックの筆先を利用して動きを大切に描きます。描いたイラストレーションをスキャニングし、“A-1”はそのままカラー出力します。“B-1”と“C-1”は、フォトショップでカラーバランスやブレの操作を1回加え、カラー出力をしたものです。“A-2”“B-2”“C-2”は、“A-1”“B-1”“C-1”をモノクロ出力し、コピックを使いそれぞれ異なる表現で描いてあります。

Here is a nude, which is somewhat more complex than the family tree. First, make a nude sketch of a woman in copic. Be careful when drawing with the pen in copic. Scan the illustration, and print it out in color as "A-1". "B-1" and "C-1" were created in Photoshop with the color balance and blur tools, and printed in color. "A-2", "B-2" and "C-2" are monochrome print-outs of "A-1", "B-1" and "C-1", with additional drawing in copic.

制作プロセス■Production Process
Original→Scan (GT-6000)→Edit / Stroke→Print out / Monochrome (MICROLINE 801PS)→Paint (COPIC)

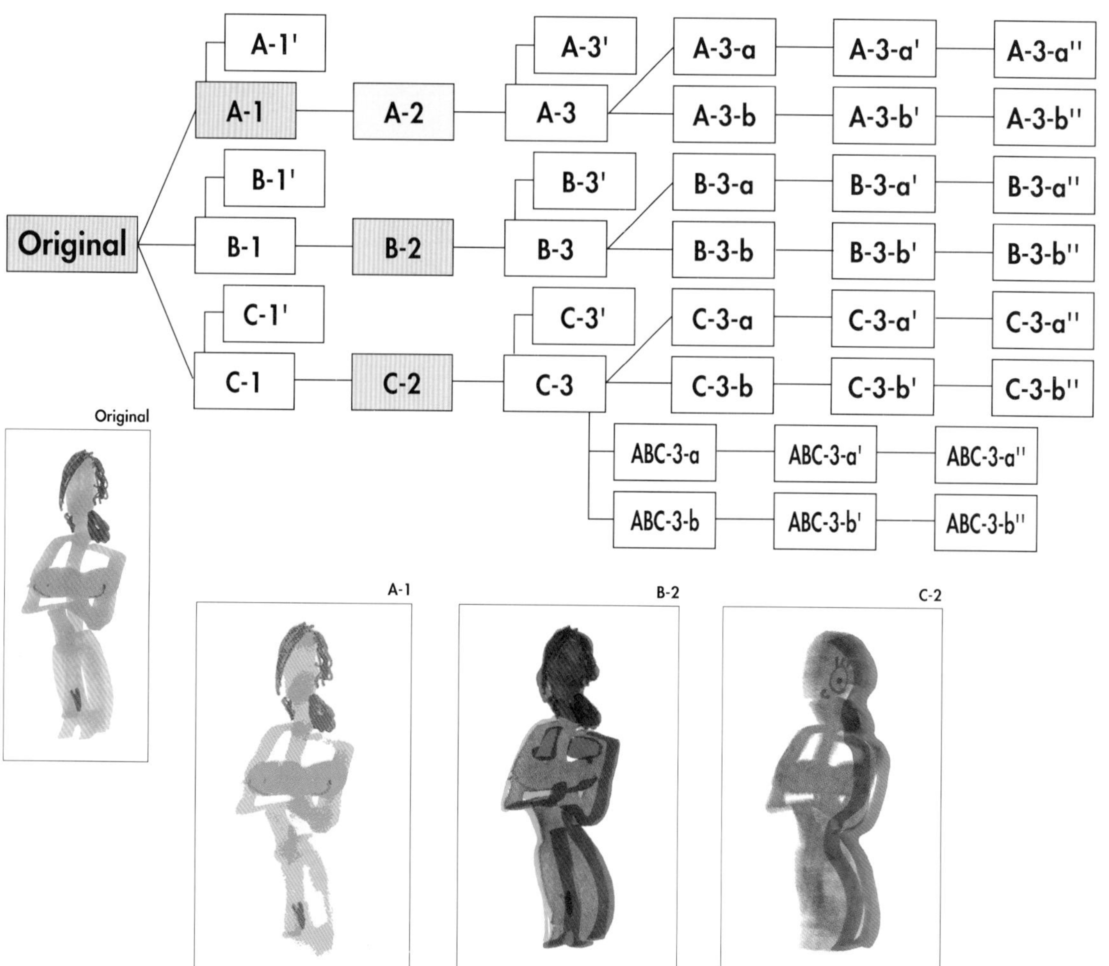

Nude B-3-a''

前ページのNudeをさらに展開します。"B-3"は、"B-2"のイラストレーションをスキャニングし、フォトショップのフィルタの水晶とモザイクの操作を加えます。"B-3"をモノクロ出力し、アナログ的操作をコピックを使ってさらに描きます。できたものが"B-3-a"で、またスキャニングし、操作を加えてできたものが"B-3-a'"でバックを黒く塗りつぶしたものが"B-3-a''"です。"B-3-b''""C-3-a''""C-3-b''"は"B-3-a''"と同じような展開を示しています。

This illustration shows further development of the nude on the previous page. "B-3" is scanned from illustration "B-2", then manipulated with Photoshop's Crystallize and Mosaic filters. It is then printed in monochrome, with further additions and positioning with analog and copic. The new work, "B-3-a", is scanned again, and filled with black background, becoming the finished work, "B-3-a''". "B-3-b''", "C-3-a''" and "C-3-b''" are developed in the same way as "B-3-a''".

制作プロセス■Production Process
Original→Scan (GT-6000)→Image / Adjust-Color Balance→Print out / Monochrome (MICROLINE 801PS)→Paint (COPIC) →Scan (GT-6000)→Filter / Stylize-Crystallize+Sharpen+Mosaic→Image / Map-Arbitrary→Print out / Monochrome (MICROLINE 801PS)→Paint (COPIC) →Scan (GT-6000)→Filter / Minimum→Image / Adjust-Color Balance→Edit / Tool-Paint Bucket→Print out / Color (PIXEL Dio)

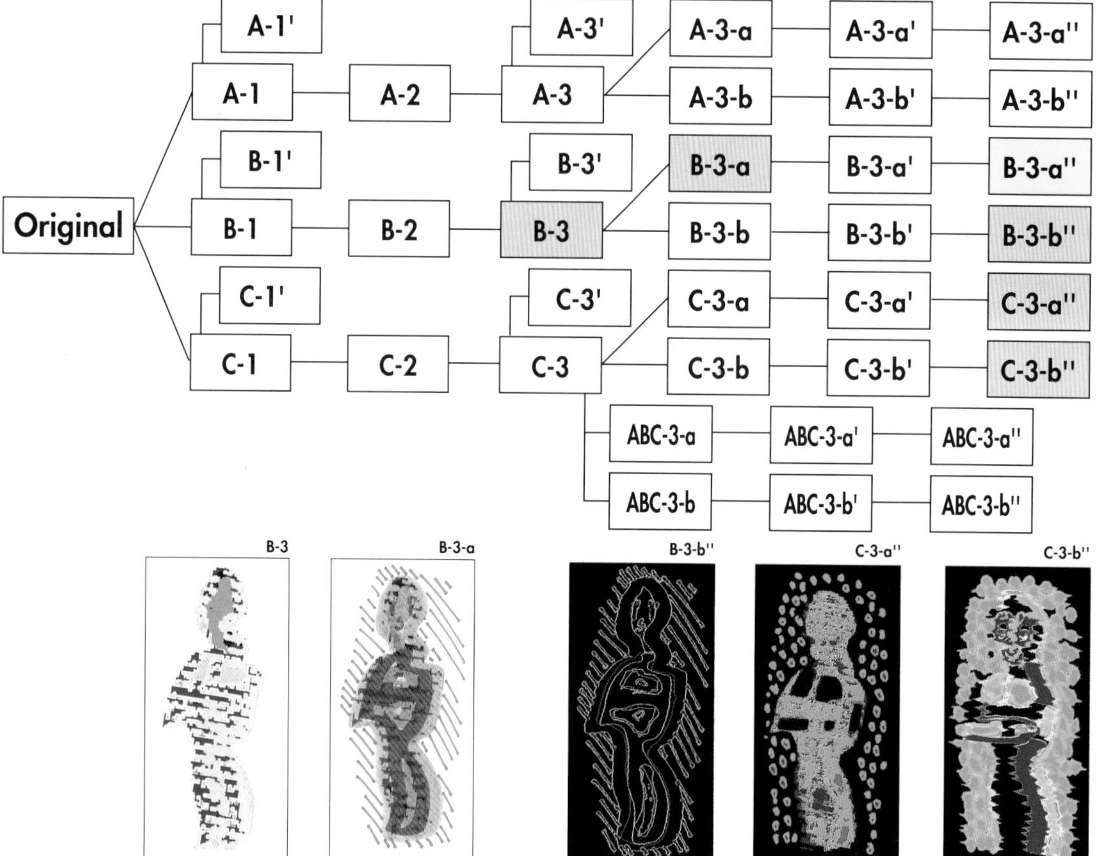

B-3　B-3-a　B-3-b''　C-3-a''　C-3-b''

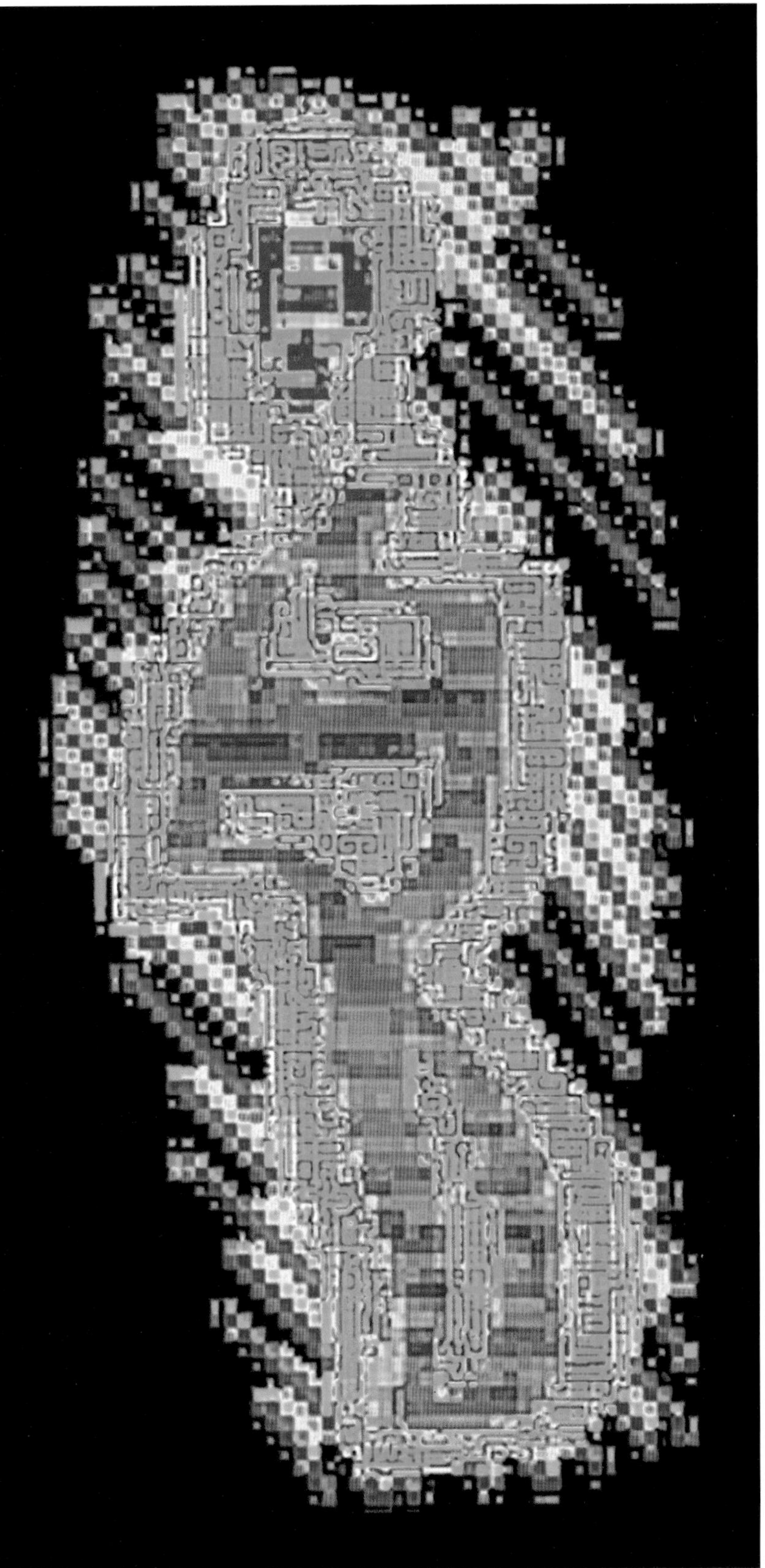

Nude ABC-3-a

ここでは、“A- 3 ”“B- 3 ”“C- 3 ”から派生した組み合わせの展開をします。それぞれの操作してあるイラストレーションを３点組み合わせモノクロ出力し、アナログ的操作をコピックを使って描き加え、新たなイラストレーションを描きます。

Shown here is a combination developed from "A-3", "B-3" and "C-3". The variously manipulated illustrations are output as a three-point set, and copic is used to add new analog configuration.

制作プロセス■Production Process
Original→Nude A-3+B-3+C-3→Print out / Monochrome (MICROLINE 801PS)→Paint (COPIC) →Scan (GT-6000)

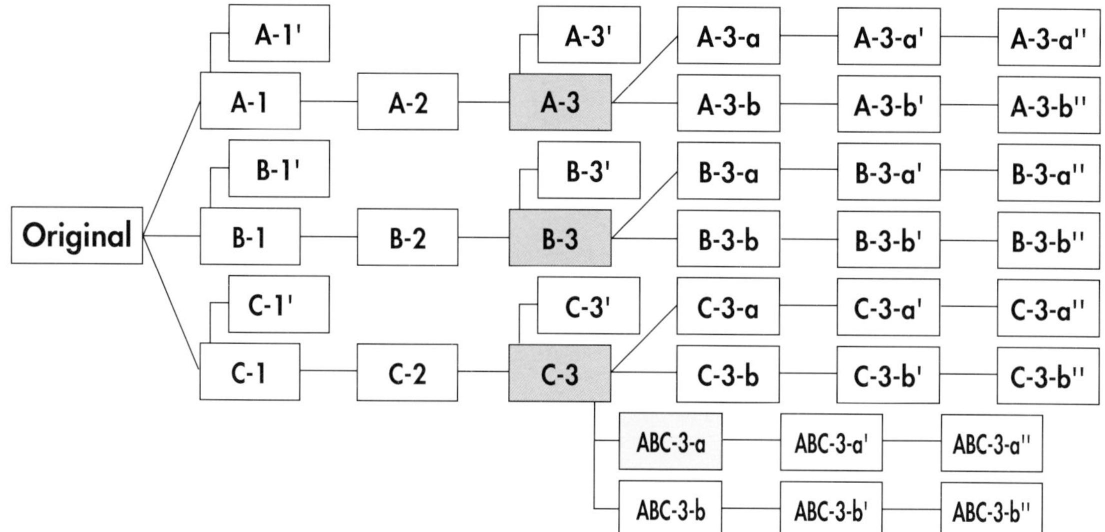

A-3

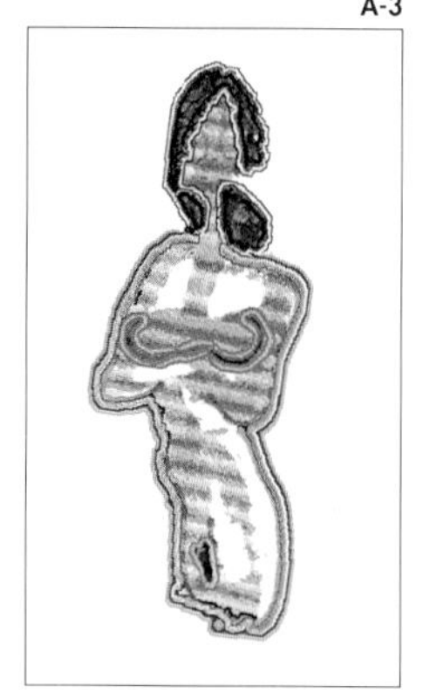

B-3

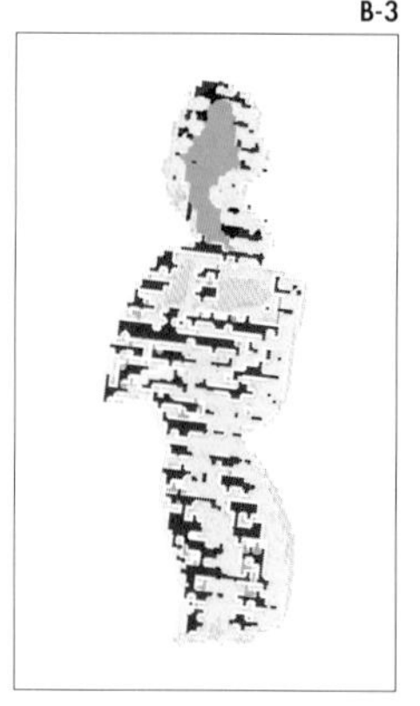

C-3

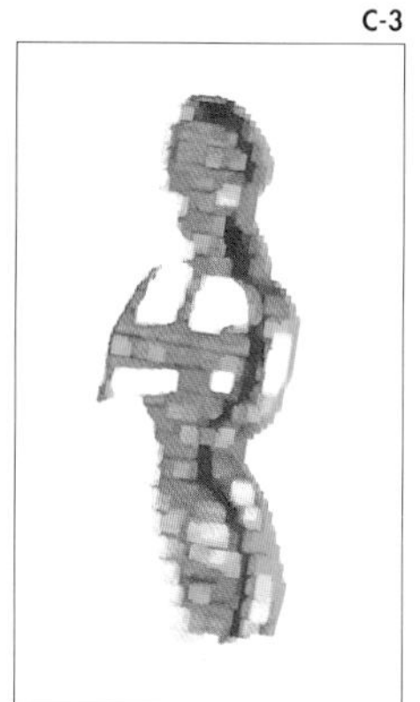

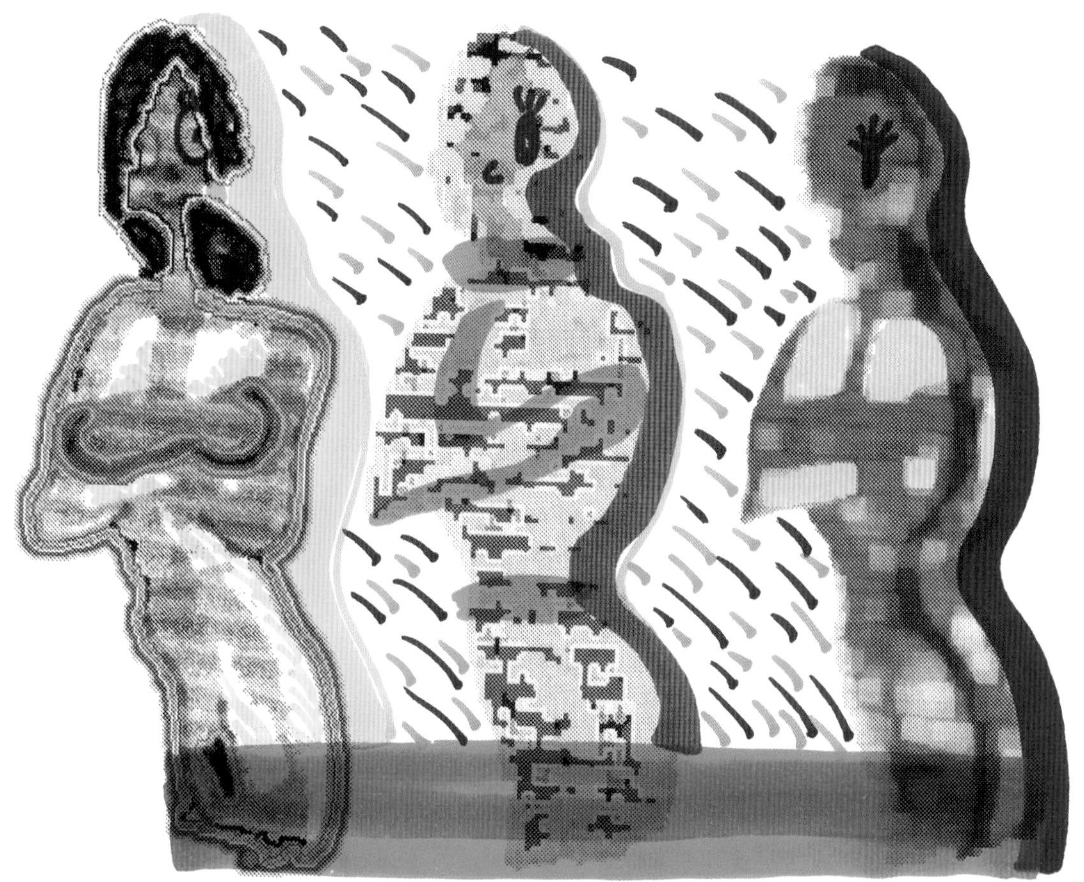

Nude ABC-3-a''

前ページのイラストレーションのつながりにさらに操作を加え、“ABC-3-a''” まで家系図的に展開し、美しいイラストレーションを表現しました。参考例として、特徴のあるイラストレーションを下に示してあります。このように、ステコン技法の家系図の考え方と展開の仕方を見ていくと、アナログ表現とデジタル表現の融合が理解できます。一番最初に描いたイラストレーションと、ステコン技法の家系図の最後にできたイラストレーションを比較すると、驚くほどの表現の広がりを見て知ることができます。

Here further development of the illustration on the proceeding page is shown. The picture is developed in the family tree-style, i.e. "ABC-3-a." For reference, the development of the illustration with these characteristics is shown below. Through this diagram of the Stacom Method the process of analog and digital work can be understood. A comparison of the first analog drawing with the final product of the Stacom Method shows a remarkable degree of development.

制作プロセス■Production Process
Original→Nude A-3+B-3+C-3→Print out / Monochrome (MICROLINE 801PS)→Paint (COPIC) →Scan (GT-6000)→Filter / Stylize-Crystallize→Image / Adjust-Hue→Edit/ Tool-Smudge→Print out / Color (PIXEL Dio)

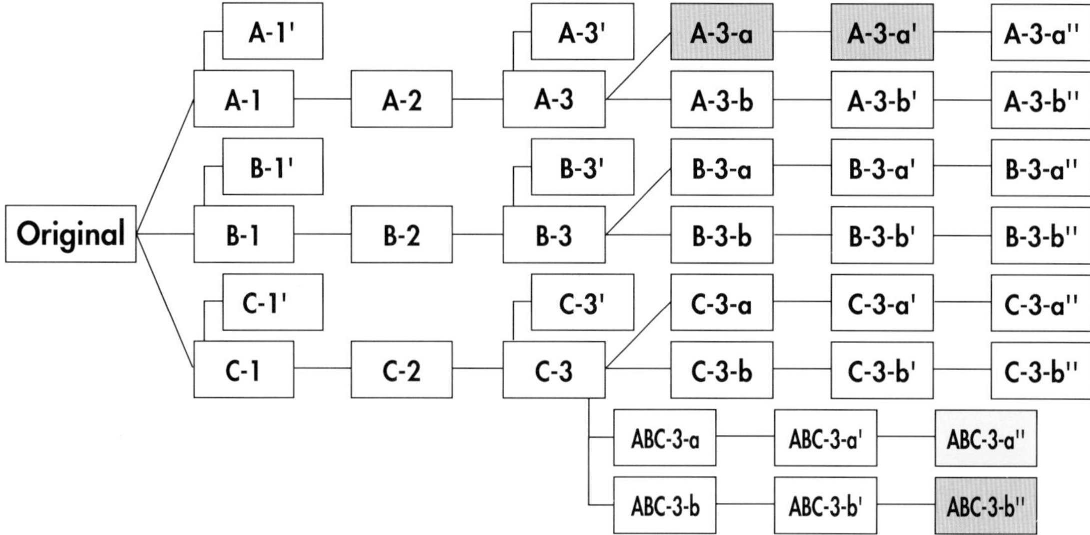

A-3-a

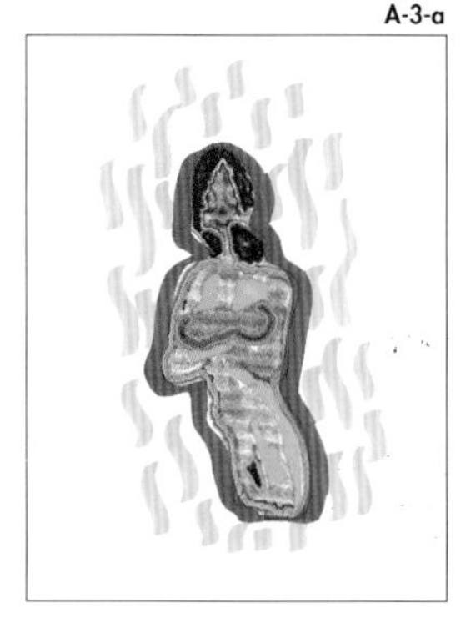

A-3-a'

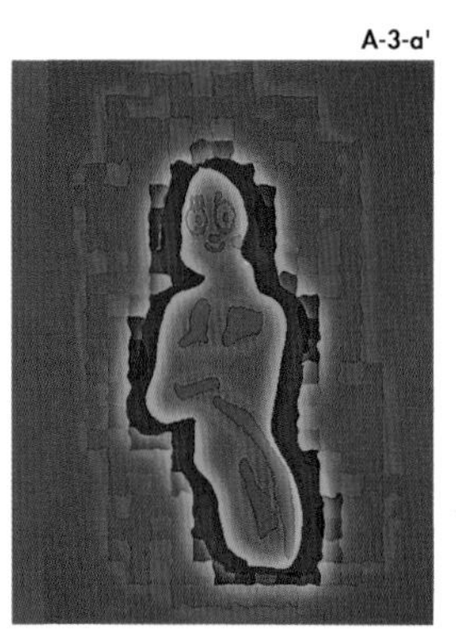

ABC-3-b''

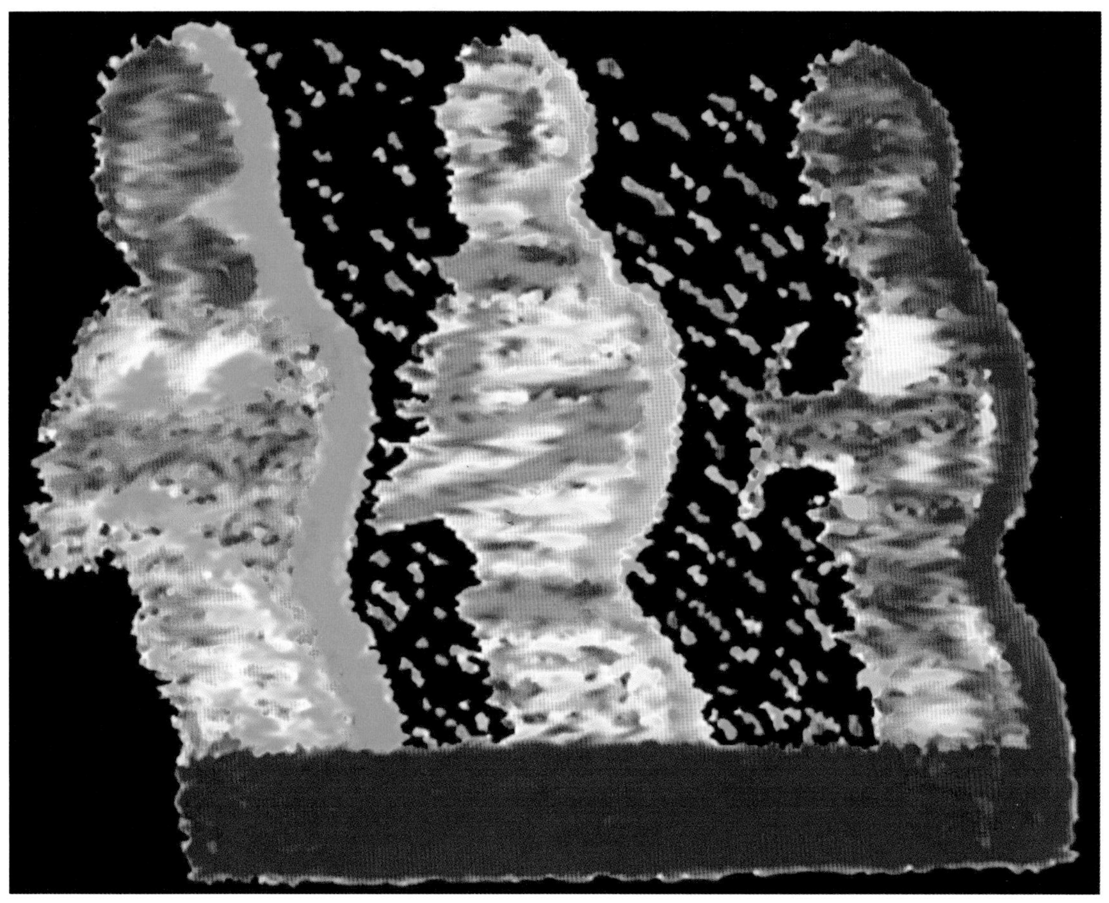

Chapter
4

W●メタモルフォーゼって、なに？
What is Metamorphose?

メタモルフォーゼ「カリカチュア」■ Metamorphose "Caricature"

メタモルフォーゼ（metamorphose）とはドイツ語で、変形、変身、変貌、変態、芸術的変質の意味を持ちます。「Peace」のポスターは、湾岸戦争（1991年）の最中、イスラエル美術館の学芸員（キュレーター）から手紙をもらい、それに触発され３点のシリーズポスターをつくりました。戦争の矛盾を告発するために、フセインとブッシュの顔をそれぞれ道化師の顔までメタモルフォーゼします。フセインがピエロにかわって、ヴィクトリーの“V”が跳ね返ってブッシュになります。マッキントッシュを導入した時に、いちばん楽で面白くて、誰もができる方法を探して作りました。フセインの顔をスキャニングして、Macのマウスを使って消しゴムツールと鉛筆ツールでデッサンをするように描いていきます。そして１枚１枚をファイルに保存しました。これをもし、１枚１枚紙に描くとしたら、大変な時間がかかってしまいますが、Macのデスクトップでは整理整頓された形で見ることが可能です。

Metamorphose is German, and means to change shape, transform, or transfigure in an artistic sense. The "Peace" poster came about as a result of a letter I received from the curator of the Israel Museum of Fine Arts during the midst of the Gulf War. I did a series of three posters, and in order to show the contradictions of war, used a metamorphosis of Hussein's and Bushes faces in one. They both become clowns in the midst of Bushes victory sign. This method is one which anyone can enjoy on a Macintosh.The faces were scanned, and the mouse was then used with the erasure tool and pencil tool to create the design. One by one, the files were created and saved. It would have taken a great deal of time if I had been drawing by hand. The Mac desktop made the arrangement you see here quite easy.

メタモルフォーゼ「共作」■ Metamorphose "Collaboration"

p.90〜p.95までの３作品は、イラストレーターの若尾真一郎さんとぼくが、『ASAhIパソコン』誌上（1992.4.1〜1993.9.15）において「電脳兄弟のパソコン放浪記」というタイトルのイラストレーションを共作したときのものです。これは、若尾真一郎さんのイラストレーションをファックスで受取りスキャニングし、そして、ぼくのイラストレーションと、Macで組み合わせ、メタモルフォーゼの手法で表現したものです。イラストレーターのこのような共作はコンピュータだからこそできることで、今後の新しい表現領域を広げました。まさにアナログとデジタルのフュージョンです。音楽でいえば、まるでジャズセッションのようです。制作プロセスは、Chapter 2 で解説した単純な手法のみで表現してありますが、デザインの切り口が異なるだけで、このようなイメージの広がりを見せます。

Take a look at the three works shown on pages 90-95. Here, illustrator Shinichiro Wakao and I created illustrations for "Electric Brain Bothers PC Diary", which ran in Asahi PC Magazine from April 1, 1992 - Sept. 15, 1993. I received Mr. Wakao's illustrations by fax, then scanned them, then combined them with my own illustrations in a digital metamorphosis. Collaborations involving illustrations are made possible by the computer, which has opened a whole new frontier in this area. It's certainly a fusion of analog and digital. If this were music, it would be a jazz session. The methods discussed in Chapter 2 are simple to understand, but with different approaches to design, the possibilities for images are endless.

M ●メタモルフォーゼ
Metamorphose

Hussein

1

2

3

6

5

4

7

8

9

M ●メタモルフォーゼ
Metamorphose

Bush

1

2

3

6

5

4

7

8

9

■－91

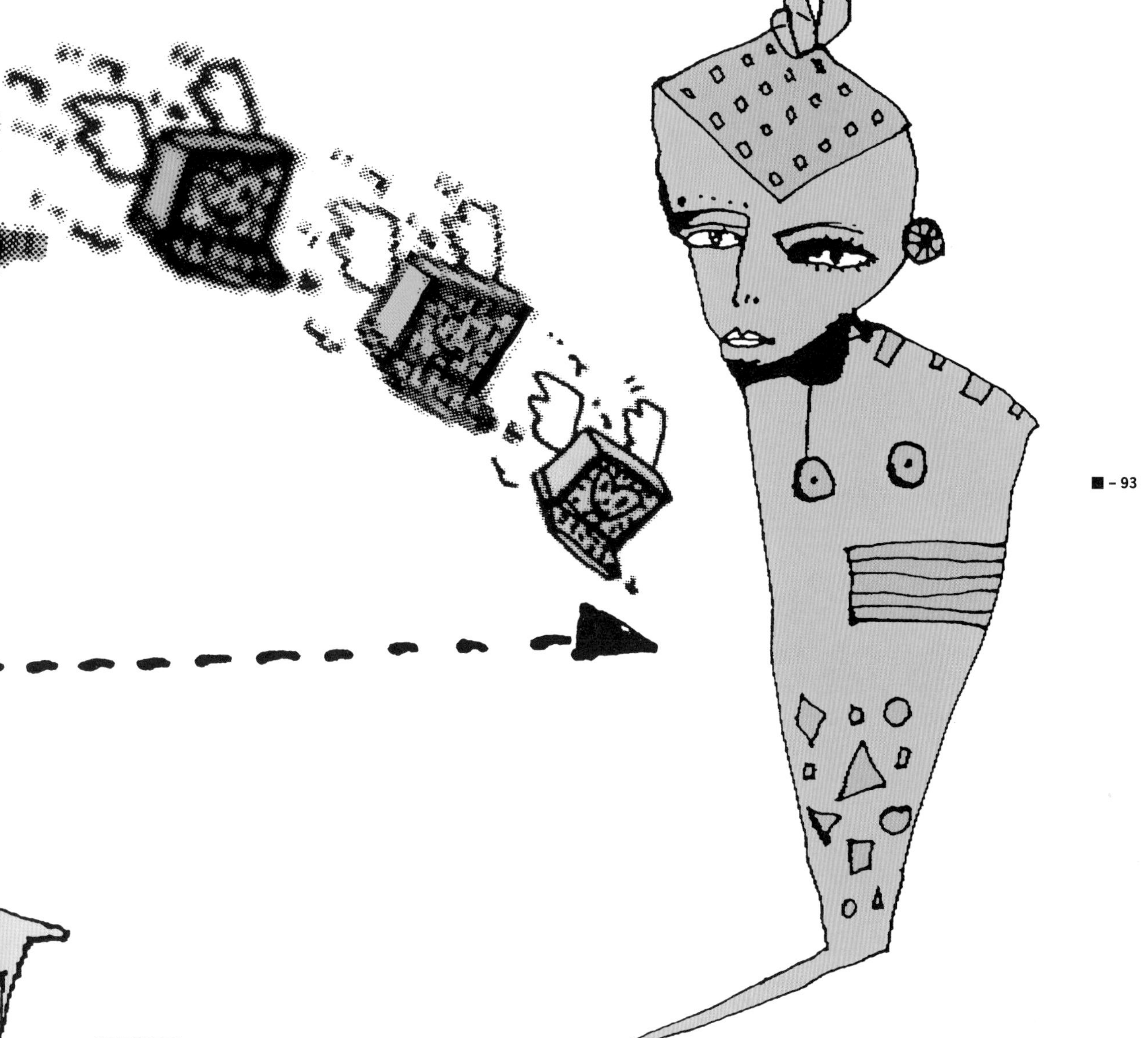

Chapter
5

W●秋山孝のMacデザインって、なに？
What is Takashi Akiyama's Mac Design Method?

ここまででChapter 1 ～ 4 までの超初級技法を学びました。ではそのつぎに秋山孝のデザイン展開を見てみましょう。技法は非常に初歩的ですが、その作者の考え方によって感性がうかがえるところが魅力的です。

イラストレーションを描くことにおいて、ここではMacを最大限に活かし、デジタル化することによって、独特な表現の変化があります。現代では、グラフィックデザインにおいても日常使う道具がコンピュータ化されてきています。コピー機もファックスも、もちろんデジタルの代表選手です。印刷技術もコンピュータ製版になり、デジタルに変換されてきています。いままでオリジナル原稿を作っていたイラストレーター達は、それを写真で複写し、四色分版してから印刷入稿していました。近頃は、ダイレクト製版に変わり、カメラで複写する必要がなくなりました。コンピュータで読み取るスキャニングの作業です。テクノロジーの発達によって、イラストレーションも表現様式やスタイルが時代とともに変化していくだろうと考えられます。

たとえば、プレゼンテーション用のスケッチを描く場合、着色することにも、Macを使うようになってきました。また、そのバリエーションもMacを使って作るようになりました。モニターを見ながら担当者やクライアントと打合せをし、考えを進め、シミュレーションします。このように近年かなり大きな変化が起きてきました。

画材においても、プレゼンテーション用の定着力の弱いマーカーも、コンピュータの出現によって、スキャンして保存ができ複製が簡単にできるため利用価値が上がりました。コンピュータは、このように新たなデザインやイラストレーション作業において、切っても切り離せないこれからの重要な道具として扱っていかなければなりません。

In Chapters 1 - 4 we learned the most basic aspects of the method. Now let's look at Takashi Akiyama's design development techniques. The method is very basic; rather, the appeal is in the different effects that each artist will produce with it.

In illustration, one can make the fullest use of a Macintosh, and with digital technology all kinds of effects can be achieved. Today, the computer is becoming an everyday tool of graphic design. Fax and copying machines are of course other full-time digital performers. Printing technology is now found in the form of computer-made film separations. Now illustrators are taking photos of original illustrations, making film separations of them, and having them printed. This is done with scanning. Along with the changing technology, illustration is evolving into a new age.

For instance, in a sketch for a presentation, color might now be added with a Mac. The creator might sit down with the client at the monitor to discuss the development using live simulation. In this way, very big changes have been taking place recently.

Now, such materials as markers, which were unreliable in presentations, can be scanned and duplicated on a Mac, making them much more valuable. Because of the support the computer offers, it is becoming more and more indispensable as a tool in design and illustration.

秋山孝の“Macイラスト講座”のカバーデザイン
Takashi Akiyama's "Getting Started as a Mac Illustrator" Cover Design

Macの特徴的な操作ツールのひとつであるマウス（ねずみ）をキャラクターデザインし、Macで表現できる神秘的な宇宙をイメージして黄色とオレンジでうずまきを作りました。そして、2つを重ね合わせ、Macの表紙にふさわしいデザインが生まれました。

A character design of a mouse, one of the unique operating tools of the Mac, superimposed on a gold and yellow spiral representing the mysterious universe that can be expressed with the Mac. From this superimposition, a design suited for the cover page was born.

1993, Offset, 257×190mm

『うずまき』ステコン技法
"Spiral" Stacom method

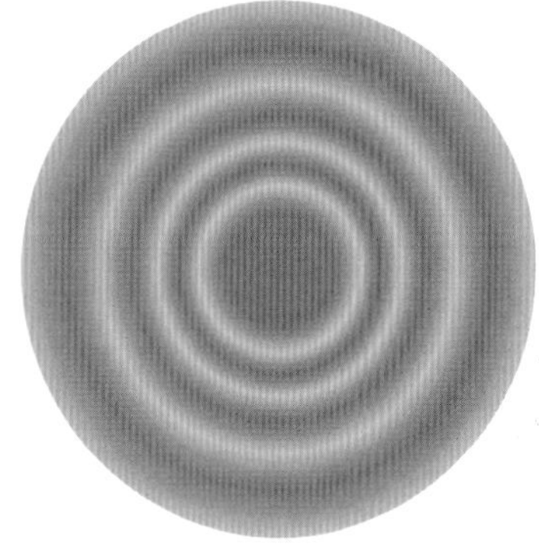

Takashi Akiyama
Getting Started as a Mac Illustrator
Welcome to Macintosh
Bowang
Click!
ISBN 4-7661-0769-1
Getting Started as a Mac Illustrator Takashi Akiyama
GRAPHIC-SHA

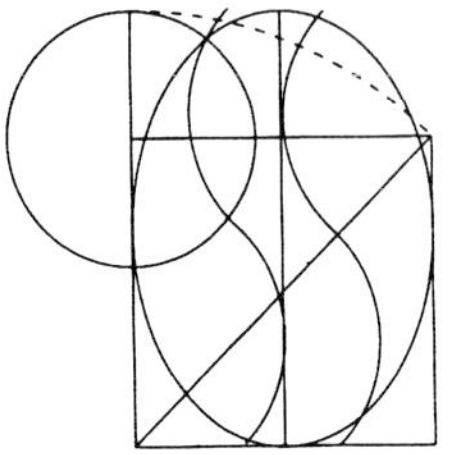

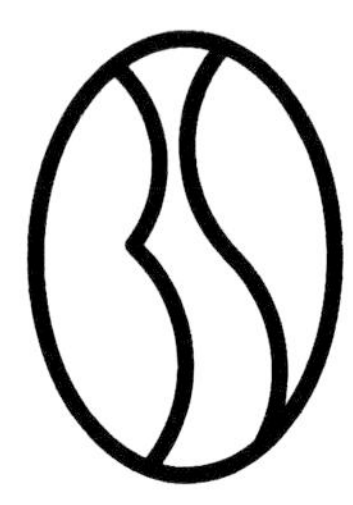

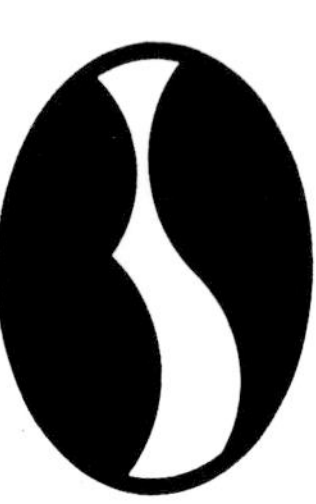

"現代の作家と弟子展"のポスター
A poster for an exhibition of "Artists and Students"

イタリアと日本の国際交流展のための告知ポスター。同展は、イタリア・ミラノにあるブレラ（BRERA）国立美術学校のナポレオンの間で開かれたました。創形美術学校（Sokei Academy of Fine Arts）とブレラ国立美術学校の交流展のためにオリジナル制作し、ブレラの頭文字の"B"と創形の"S"、さらにイタリアと日本のイメージを黄金比率の美しさの中におさめ、これからの芸術における永遠の交流を象徴しデザインしたものです。

An advertisement for an exhibition of Italian and Japanese exchange. The exhibition took place in Milano's Brera National Art Institute. Sokei Academy of Fine Arts was the Japanese participant. The image uses the "B" of Brera and the "S" of Sokei in a mixture of yellow and gold which symbolizes Japan and Italy, and looks forward to eternal exchange between the two countries.

1992, Silkscreen, 728×515mm

『現代の作家と弟子展』リーフレット
"Artists and Students" Leaflet

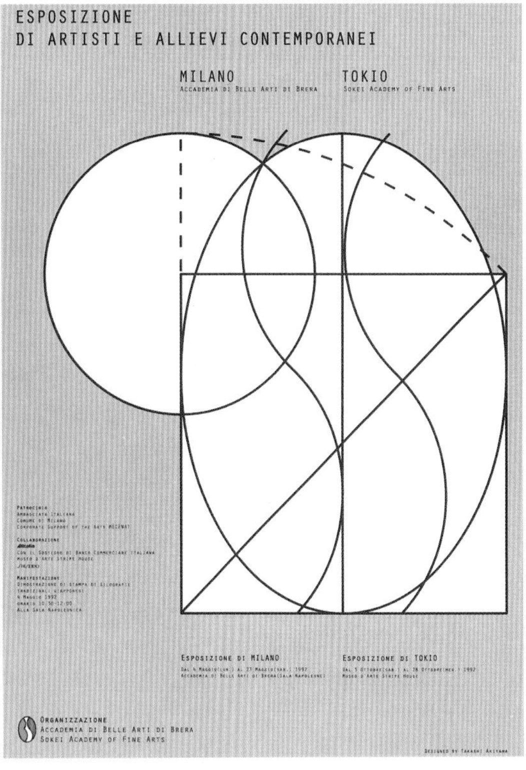

ESPOSIZIONE

DI ARTISTI E ALLIEVI CONTEMPORANEI

SOKEI ACADEMY OF FINE ARTS

ESPOSIZIONE DI MILANO / DAL 4 MAGGIO(LUN.) AL 23 MAGGIO(SAB.)1992 ACCADEMIA DI BELLE ARTI DI BRERA (SALA NAPOLEONE)

ESPOSIZIONE DI TOKIO / DAL 3 OTTOBRE (SAB.) AL 28 OTTOBRE (MER.)1992 MUSEO D'ARTE STRIPE HOUSE

MILANO

TOKIO

ACCADEMIA DI BELLE ARTI DI BRERA

ORGANIZZAZIONE
ACCADEMIA DI BELLE ARTI DI BRERA
SOKEI ACADEMY OF FINE ARTS

PATROCINIO
AMBASCIATA ITALIANA
COMUME DI MILANO
CORPORATE SUPPORT OF THE ARTS MÉCÉNAT

COLLABORAZIONE
Alitalia
CON IL SOSTEGNO DI BANCA COMMERCIARE ITALIANA
MUSEO D'ARTE STRIPE HOUSE
SHISEIDO

MANIFESTAZIONE
DIMOSTRAZIONE DI STAMPA DI XILOGRAFIE
TRADIZINALI GIAPPONESI
4 MAGGIO 1992
ORARIO 10:30~12:00
ALLA SALA NAPOLEONICA

DESIGNED BY TAKASHI AKIYAMA

『コンドームくんとエイズウイルスくん』キャラクター
"Condom Boy and AIDS Virus Boy" Characters

"秋山孝のコンドームくんとエイズウイルスくん展" のポスター
A poster for "Takashi Akiyama Exhibition Condom Boy and AIDS Virus Boy"

ストップエイズキャンペーンの個展告知ポスター。同展は1992年5月14日から5月26日、渋谷のガーディアンガーデンでおこない、入場者数は約3260人でした。テレビ、雑誌などに数多く取り上げられ、日本で初めて個人がおこなったエイズに関するキャンペーンとして話題になりました。シンボルマークはインターナショナルに理解できるように、禁止の記号とエイズという手描き文字を組み合わせています。また、ストップエイズの主役はコンドームくんで、コンドームのマイナスイメージを払い、プラスイメージへ転換することを目的に、もっとも有効な手段としてコンドームをキャラクター化し、生命のいぶきを与えました。

A poster for an individual exhibition in the "Stop AIDS Campaign." The exhibit was held in Shibuya's Guardian Garden from May 5 to 26, 1992. 3260 people attended, and the exhibit was reported widely in news and television. As the first individual AIDs campaign in Japan the exhibit won wide attention.The symbol mark is formed of the globally-recognized, hand-drawn stop sign and AIDs letters. The Condom Boy image was designed to dispel the negative image of the condom and replace it with a positive image. Making the condom into a living character was the most effective way of doing this.

1992, Offset, 1030×728mm

『ストップエイズ キャンペーン』 シール
"STOP AIDS Campaign" Seal

『ストップエイズ キャンペーン』 バッジ
"STOP AIDS Campaign" Badge

TAKASHI AKIYAMA EXHIBITION · 11:00~21:00 (5.20.Wednesday Closed) · CONDOM BOY AND AIDSVIRUS BOY · 1992.5.14.Thursday.~5.26.Tuesday.
AIDS
CONDOM BOY
Guardian Garden
1F RISE BLDG. 13-17 UDAGAWACHO,SHIBUYA-KU,TOKYO 150 TEL.03-5489-5454 FAX. 03-5489-5455
SUPPORT:TAKEO COMPANY LTD. OKAMOTO INDUSTRIES,INC. COOPERATION:DAI NIPPON PRINTING CO.,LTD.

『LOVE MOTHER EARTH』タイトルロゴ
"LOVE MOTHER EARTH" Title Logo

LOVE
MOTHER
EARTH

"LOVE MOTHER EARTH（人間）" のポスター
A poster for "Love Mother Earth (Human)"

"LOVE MOTHER EARTH" というテーマで、セントラル美術館にて環境保護をテーマとしたポスター展が開かれました。タイトルが「スーパーデザイニング展 2（デザインが変える、日本を変える）」で、おもにコンピュータを使って表現の領域を広げるためのものであり、その特徴を最大限にいかしたイラストレーションとデザインが発表されました。この作品は、10点シリーズのひとつで骨格シリーズと呼び、絶滅の危機を骨で象徴化しています。地球のグリーンと目のグリーンは自然の美しさをあらわします。

Under the "Love Mother Earth" theme a poster exhibit was held at the Central Museum to promote environmental protection. The title of the event was "Super Designing; Changing Design, Changing Japan" and for the most part it focused on expanding the possibilities of computer design. Designs and illustrations were very avant-garde. This poster was one in a series of ten. The bones suggest the crisis of extinction, while the green of the eyes and surroundings recall the beauty of nature.

1991, Offset, 1030×728mm

『LOVE MOTHER EARTH（鳥）』ステコン技法
"LOVE MOTHER EARTH (bird)" Stacom method

『LOVE MOTHER EARTH（魚）』ポスター, オフセット
"LOVE MOTHER EARTH (Fish)" Poster, 1991, Offset, 728×, 1030mm

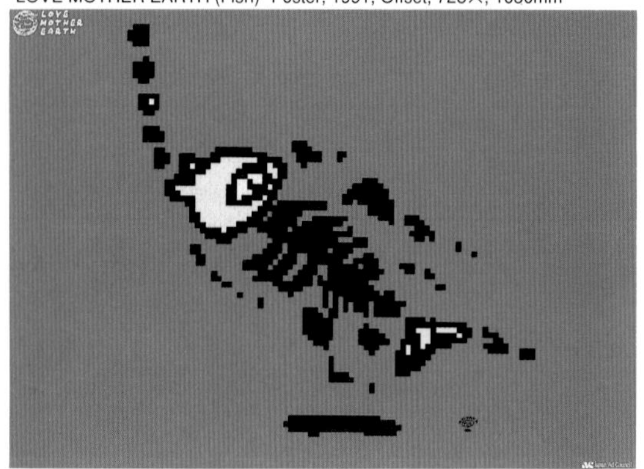

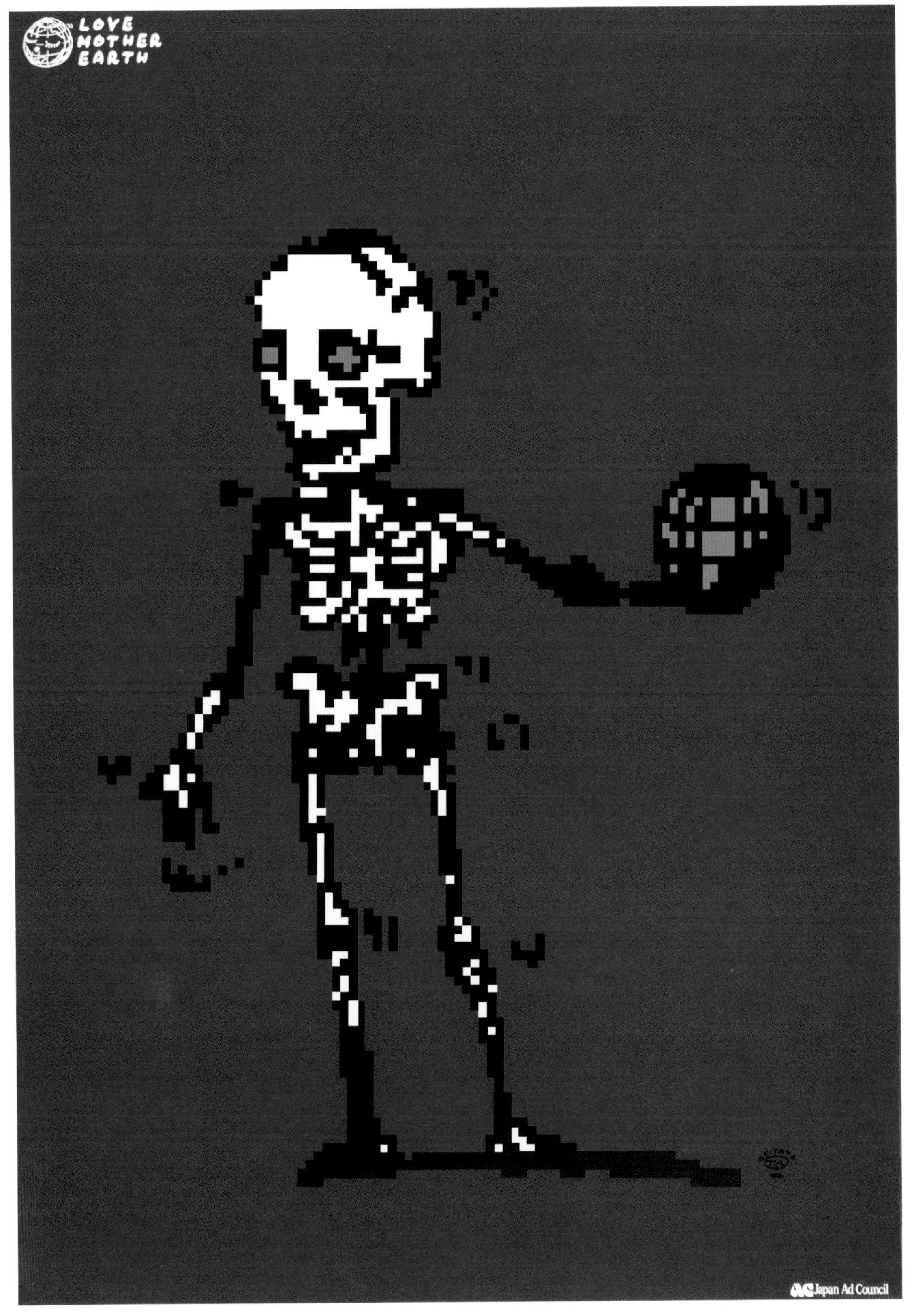
LOVE
MOTHER
EARTH
AKIYAMA
Japan Ad Council

『ユーモアの星』オリジナルイラストレーション
"Star of Humor" Original Illustration

“第５回ユーモア広告大賞”のカタログ
A catalog for "The 5th Humor Advertising Contest"

読売新聞社主催の新聞広告におけるコンクール「ユーモア広告大賞」のためのカタログ。秋山孝のステコン技法を利用したイラストレーションを表紙に使い、デザインしています。タイトルを「輝け！ユーモアの星」とし、ポスターからカタログデザインへと展開していきました。第１回から現在までアートディレクションを担当しています。

This is a catalog for the Humor Advertising Contest, sponsored by the Yomiuri Newspaper. The example here, used on the cover, employed the Akiyama Stacom method.
It says: "Shine. The Humor Star," taking the reader from the cover to the inside. Akiyama has supervised the catalog since its first edition.

1991, Offset, 297×210mm

『第４回ユーモア広告大賞』カタログ
"The 4th Humor Advertising Contest" Catalog

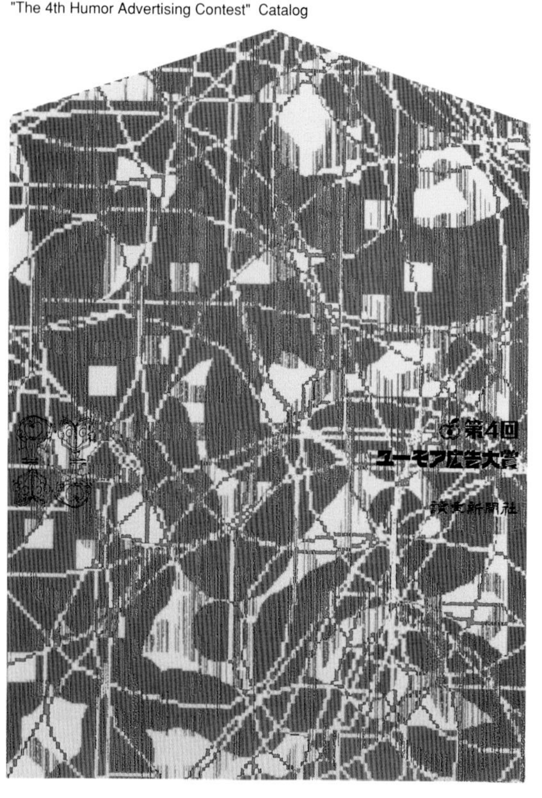

■ - 107

『地球』オリジナルイラストレーション
"Earth" Original Illustration

"The 3rd ASEAN Cartoonist Exhibition"のカタログ
A catalog for "The 3rd ASEAN Cartoonist Exhibition"

第３回アセアン漫画家展のためのカタログ。アセアン発足25周年記念事業で、国際交流基金アセアン文化センターが主催、「漫画にみる各国の都市事情」というサブタイトルでした。アセアン各国の５人の漫画家の展覧会です。このカタログのメインビジュアルにはステコン技法を用い、別版でシアン、マゼンタ、イエロー、ブラックをハーフトーンスクリーン設定によってモノクロ出力し、それを印刷のための版下原稿として使用しています。

The Third Asian Cartoonist's Exhibition catalog. Marking the 25th year since the founding of ASEAN, and sponsored by the ASEAN Cultural Exchange Center Foundation, it addressed the sub-subject of member nation cities. Five cartoonists from each of the five member nations entered the exhibit. Here again the main visual for the catalog utilized the Stacom method, with separate film for cyan, magenta, yellow and black set at halftone screen output, and later used as a paste-up for printing.

1992, Offset, 297×210mm

『地図』ステコン技法
"Map" Stacom method

The3rd ASEAN
Cartoonist
Exhibition

『彫刻の鳥』ステコン技法
"Sculpture Birds" Stacom method

“ユーモア彫刻展1991” のカタログ
A catalog for "1991 Humor Sculpture Exhibition "

日本初のユーモアをテーマとした彫刻の公募展のためのカタログ。作品は船橋にあるワンパク王国で展示されました。ユーモアは、言葉や生活環境、世代の違いを超えた世界共通の「感性」であり、「ことば」であると考えています。このカタログの表現技法は、The 3rd ASEAN Cartoonist Exhibitionのカタログと同じように、ハーフトーンスクリーン設定でバックの部分をつくり、キャラクターは35mmポジ（ステコン技法）で製版工程ではめ込みました。

A catalog for Japan's first open humor sculpture contest. Entries were shown at Funabashi's Wanpaku Park. Humor goes beyond language and living, and generational differences, and is understood across cultures. It is a matter of words and feelings. Like the ASEAN Cartoonist's Exhibition Catalog, this cover design uses 35mm film, the Stacom method and film separations for printing.

1991, Offset, 297×225mm

『美の女神ビーナス』ステコン技法
" Venus, Goddess of Beauty " Stacom method

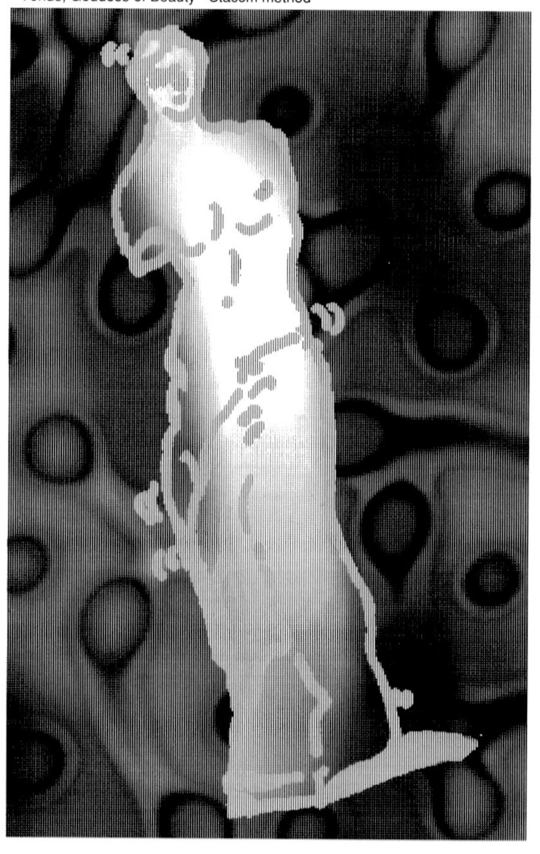

『美の女神ビーナス』オリジナルイラストレーション
" Venus, Goddess of Beauty " Original Illustration

ユーモア
彫刻展
1991
HUMOR 1991
SCULPTURE
EXHIBITION

『地球は笑う』シンボルキャラクター
"The Earth Laugh" Symbol Character

"The Best Cartoons of Nippon '92" のカタログ
A catalog for "The Best Cartoons of Nippon '92"

大宮市ユーモアセンター設立準備実行委員会発足により、大宮市がユーモア文化交流の拠点としてThe Best Cartoons of Nippon '92のカタログを発行しました。国際的なネットワーキングを象徴するために、地球のキャラクターに、Macの特徴の虹表現（ステコン技法）を使ってイラストレーションをつくりました。タイトルロゴにも虹表現を使っています。

The Preparatory Committee for the Establishment of Omiya City Humor Center published the Best Cartoons of Nippon, 1992, as part of its cultural exchange program. Symbolizing international networking, the rainbow colors of the Mac were used in the Stacom method to produce the design. The logo title also uses the rainbow hues.

1992, Offset, 297×210mm

『The Best Cartoons of Nippon '92』ポスター, オフセット
"The Best Cartoons of Nippon '92" Poster, 1992, Offset, 728×515mm

The Best Cartoons of Nippon'92

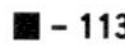

『仁王像・うん』オリジナルイラストレーション
"Nioh Omm statue" Original Illustration

“ユーモア彫刻展1992” のポスター
A poster for "1992 Humor Sculpture Exhibition".

ポスターのイラストレーションは、東大寺南大門の仁王像です。この寄せ木作りの造形は、鎌倉期の代表作として知られています。1991年に、800年目の解体修理が行われました。山口県の檜を使い、2918個の寄せ木からできています。表情は『あ、うん』の「うん」からなり、非常にユーモアを感じさせ、シンボライズした創作者の内面の豊かさをうかがいしることができます。

This poster illustration is of the Nioh statue at the South Gate of Todai-ji Temple. This famous wooden carving is a representative work of the Kamakura period. In 1991, restoration work was done on the 800 year old image. 2918 pieces of Yamaguchi prefecture cypress went into the work. The expression on the face represents the "aa-omm" utterance in a humorous fashion. The rich feelings of the original creator are fairly obvious in this work.

1992, Offset, 728×515mm

『ユーモア彫刻展1992』カタログ
"1992 Humor Sculpture Exhibition" Catalog

『仁王像・うん』ステコン技法
"Nioh Omm statue" Original Illustration

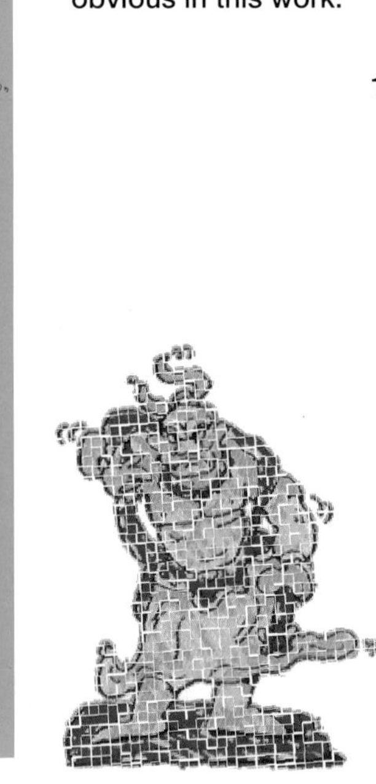

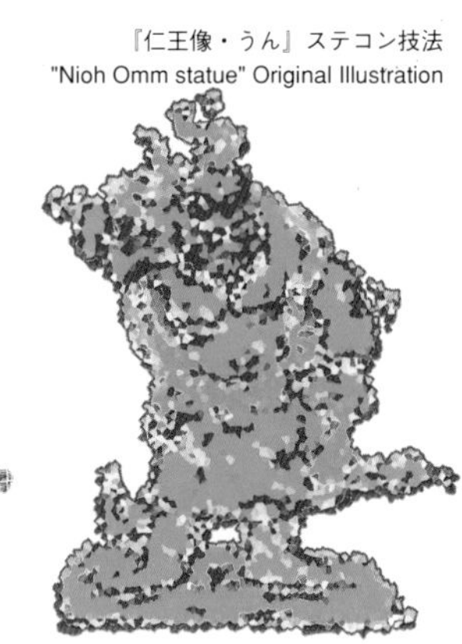

ユーモア彫刻展 1992
HUMOR 1992
SCULPTURE
EXHIBITION
アンデルセン公園
ワンパク王国
船橋市豊富町6
0474-57-6627
★応募資格
不問
★出展料
無料 ただし搬入・搬出費用は出展者の
自己負担。
★応募締切
1992年9月30日
★賞・賞金
最優秀賞（1点） 100万円（買上げ賞）
優秀賞 （1点） 30万円（買上げ賞）
奨励賞 （1点） 20万円（買上げ賞）
佳作 （5点） 各5万円
★搬入・搬出
搬入日 1992年10月27日〜29日
（AM10：00〜PM4：00）
搬出日 1992年11月10日〜11日
（AM10：00〜PM4：00）
※搬入・搬出費用は出展者の自己負担とし、直接搬入のこと。
★審査員
久里洋二（イラストレーター）
六角鬼丈（建築家）
牧野圭一（漫画家）
秋山孝（グラフィックデザイナー）
酒井清一（造形作家）
★展覧会
1992年11月1日〜11月8日
AM10：00〜PM4：00
★会場
〒274 千葉県船橋市豊富町6番地
ワンパク王国
★版権
専用版権は（財）船橋市公園協会に帰属する。
★主催
（財）船橋市公園協会、船橋市レクリエーションレジャー友の会、ユーモア彫刻展実行委員会・日本ユーモアネットワーク
★後援（予定）
船橋市教育委員会、NHK千葉放送局
★お問い合わせ・応募要項請求先
（財）船橋市公園協会
TEL 0474-35-3851 FAX 0474-35-3050

『地球くん』ステコン技法
" Earth Boy" Stacom method

“時代（いま）”の版画
A graphic art for "Age"

1991年ガーディアンガーデンでおこなわれた展覧会『時代（いま）』に出品した作品で、ステコン技法の実験を試みました。地球をキャラクター化したイラストレーションとNASAのスペースシャトルを重ね合わせ、『エコロジーとテクノロジーの共存』をビジュアル化しました。

Here is a work submitted to the 1991 Guardian Garden "Now" exhibit. The Stacom method is employed in this work. A personified world and the symbol of NASA are combined to visually symbolize "Ecology and Technology in Harmony".

1991, Offset, 500×500mm

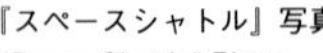
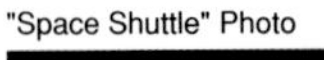

『スペースシャトル』写真
"Space Shuttle" Photo

『I'm here（霊長類）』ポスター, シルクスクリーン
"I'm here (primates)" Poster, Silkscreen, 1030×758mm

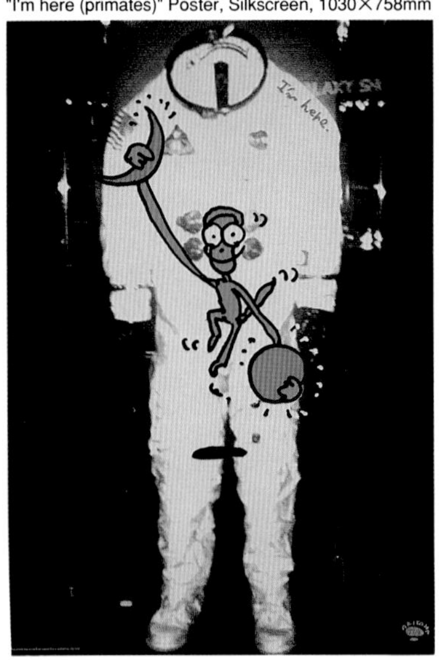

USA
NASA

『一つ目フクロウ』オリジナルキャラクター
" One-eyed owl" Original Character

“秋山孝の遊鳥展”のリーフレット
A leaflet for "Takashi Akiyama's Bird Art Exhibition"

　1993年5月20日、札幌西友西町店オープン記念にあわせ開催された展覧会『秋山孝の遊鳥展』のためのリーフレット。Macで作った虹の輝きをバックに配し、デザインしました。この虹は、コンピュータ独特の表現でデジタルの美しさの代表だと思っています。

This leaflet was produced for "Takashi Akiyama's Bird Art Exhibition" which was held to commemorate the opening of the Seiyu Nishimachi branch store in Sapporo on 20 May, 1993. It was designed with a shimmering rainbow, produced on the Mac, as a background. This rainbow represents the beauty of digital form in a way that only a computer can.

1993, Offset, 297×210mm

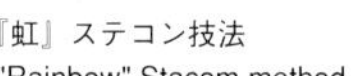

『虹』ステコン技法
"Rainbow" Stacom method

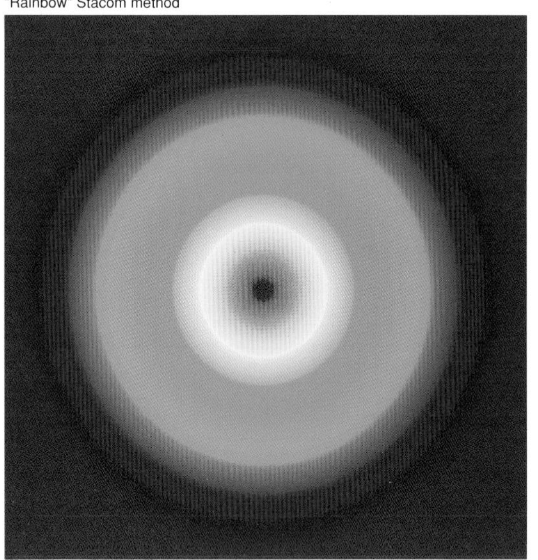

『ワンパクっ子さつきつつじまつり』ポスター, オフッセト
"WANPAKU Kid's Azalea Festival" Poster, 1992, Offset, 364×515mm

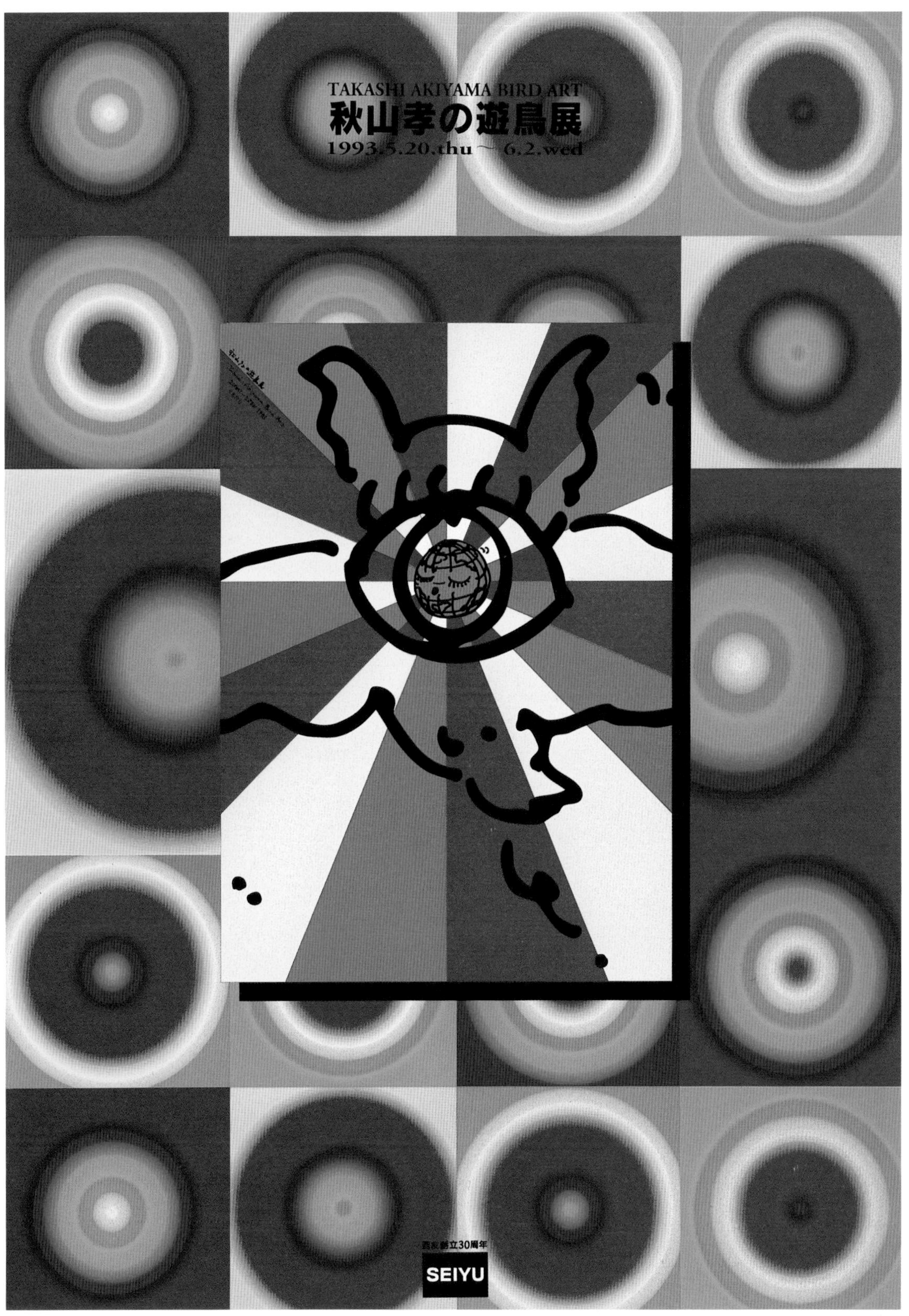
TAKASHI AKIYAMA BIRD ART
秋山孝の遊鳥展
1993.5.20.thu ~ 6.2.wed
西友創立30周年
SEIYU

『一つ目フクロウ』オリジナルキャラクター
" One-eyed owl" Original Character

“秋山孝の遊鳥展”のポスター
A poster for "Takashi Akiyama's Bird Art Exhibition"

展覧会告知ポスターで、一つ目フクロウのキャラクターをアウトラインでトレースし、コピー&ペーストのくりかえし効果を活かしたデザインを試みました。同じキャラクターをくりかえしたり、重ね合わせたりすることもコンピュータならではのデザインといえます。この作品の場合は、エコロジーの象徴である樹を一つ目フクロウの輪郭の軌跡であらわしています。

In the poster advertising this exhibition, the owl outline of the one-eyed is copied and pasted repeatedly. The copying and overlapping of the same character is a design feature that is readily associated with the computer. In this picture, a tree, the symbol of ecology is shown in the path of the one-eyed owl.

1993, Silkscreen, 1030×728mm

『The Great Characters-1』作品集
"The Great Characters-1" My portfolio

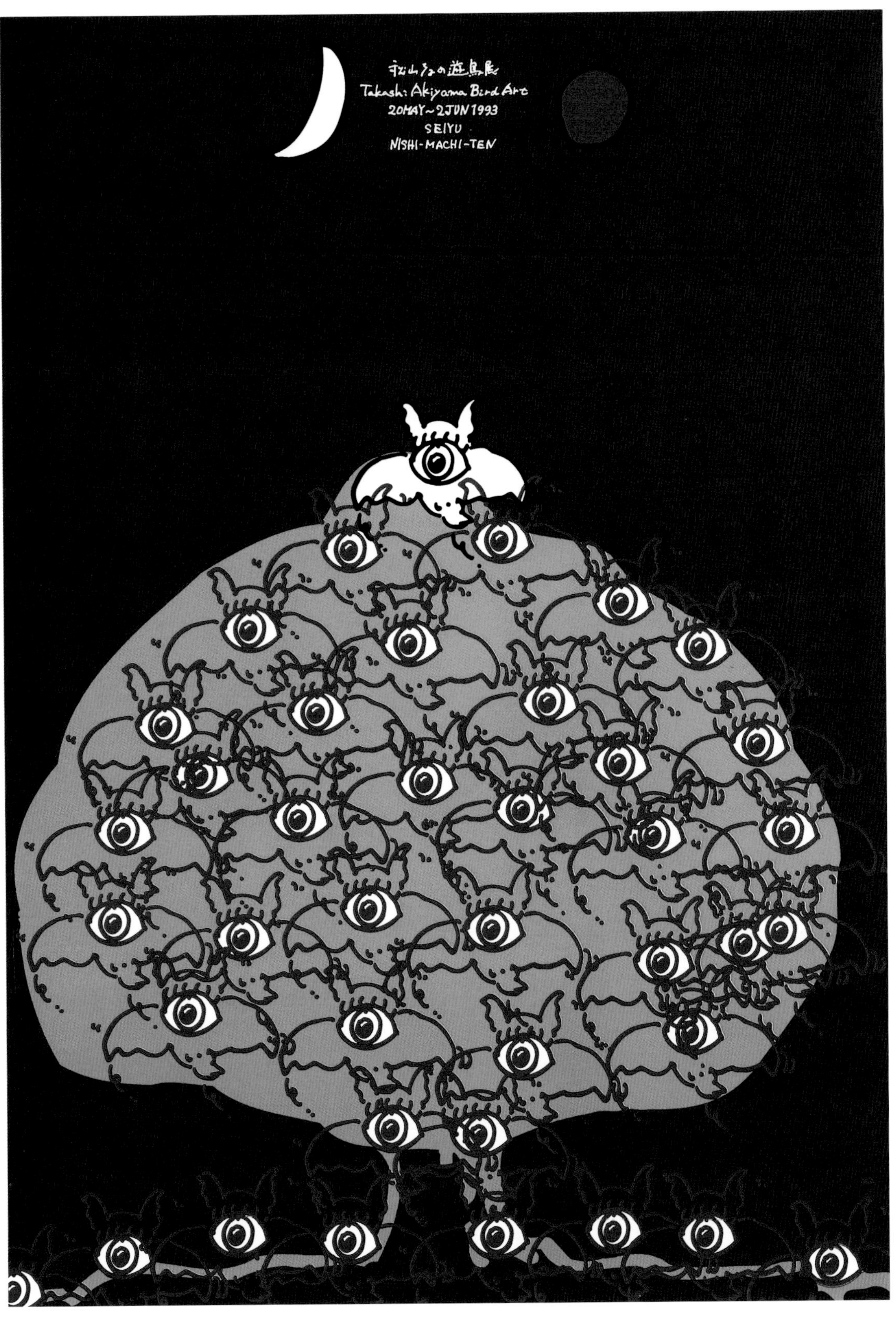
Takashi Akiyama Bird Art
20MAY~2JUN 1993
SEIYU
NISHI-MACHI-TEN

『ビリー』キャラクター
" Billy" Character

“ビリーベアのもりへいこうよ”のCD-ROM
A CD-ROM for "Let's Go to Billy Bear's Forest"

ステコン技法の展開としてのマルチメディアCD-ROM。CD-ROMは、コンピュータの外部記憶装置のひとつ。音楽用のCDと同じメディアを、読みだし専用の記憶装置に利用したものです。大量の音声や動画を必要とするマルチメディア分野での利用が注目されています。『ビリーベアのもりへいこうよ』は、絵と音と物語がひとつになった子供たちの豊かな可能性をはぐくむ新しい情操・知育ソフトです。

This multi-media CD-ROM is a further development of the Stacom method. CD-ROM is one of the many memory forms available for the computer, and it is used to store information that can be read back later in the same way as musical CD's store music. Its use is receiving a lot of attention because of its ability to store the large volumes of audio and visual data necessary in the multi-media field. "Let's Go to Billy Bear's Forest" is a new kind of educational and entertainment software that combines picture, sound and story to develop the great potential of our children.

1993, CD-ROM for Macintosh

『ビリー・ベアのもりへいこうよ』CD-ROM
"Let's Go to Billy Bear's Forest" CD-ROM

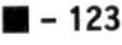

添付のフロッピーディスクについて

W● なぜ、フロッピーディスクをつけたの？
Why did you include a floppy disk in the book?

この本は、紙の上にインクで印刷された情報──紙情報です。フロッピーディスクは、紙情報とは違い、コンピュータの情報が磁気体を塗布したプラスチックの薄い円盤にデータを電磁的に記録されるデジタル情報です。それで、紙情報とデジタル情報（フロッピーディスク情報）の違いを確認し、その魅力を知るためにフロッピーディスクを付けました。その違いと魅力とは、Macのモニター上で見るイラストレーションの色の輝きです。それがステコン技法と名付けたゆえんです。

"Getting Started as a Mac Illustrator"
『秋山孝のMacイラスト講座』 Sample Data Disk

3.5" 2HD／Macintosh フォーマット　フロッピーディスク

◎ディスクの内容
1. Picture-p.27..........................32K　Illustrator／EPSFフォーマット
2. Picture-p.49........................767K　Photoshop／PICTフォーマット

◎動作環境
このSample Dataの観賞のためには、Macintosh のハードウエアが必要です。Macintoshのほとんどの機種で表示できますが、画像自体は256色表示を基本に作られています。実際にMacintoshの画面で確認することで、紙の上では把握できなかった色の情報が正確につかむことができます。

◎操作法方
まず、グラフィックソフトを起動して、ファイルオープンコマンドをプルダウンメニューから選び、見たいファイルを選択して下さい。

About attached Floppy disk

W ●なぜ、フロッピーディスクをつけたの？
hy did you include a floppy disk in the book?

The information in this book is in the form of ink printed on paper, or so-called paper information. The floppy disk is different from paper information; it is digital information electromagnetically recorded on a thin plastic disc that has been treated with a magnetic coat. I have attached this floppy disk so that people can see the difference between paper information and digital information and understand its charm. This difference and its appeal can be seen in the shimmering colors of the illustrations as they appear on the Mac monitor screen. This is the reason I chose to name this technique Stacom (stained glass and computer).

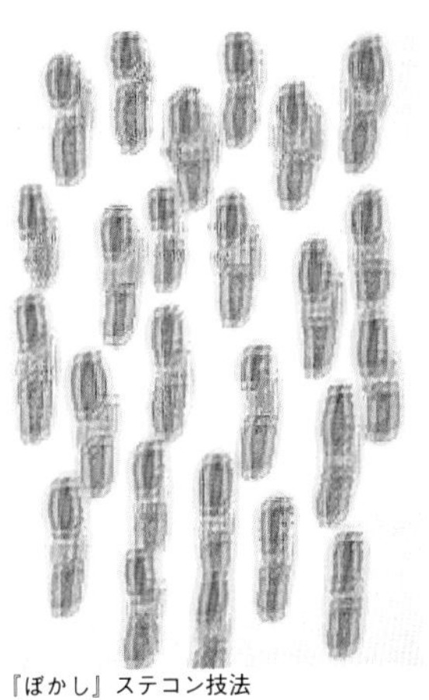

『ぼかし』ステコン技法
"Shading" Stacom method

"Getting Started as a Mac Illustrator"
『秋山孝のMacイラスト講座』 Sample Data Disk

3.5" 2HD／Macintosh-format floppy disk

◎Disk contents

1. Picture-p.27................................32 K Illustrator／EPSF format
2. Picture-p.49............................ 767 K Photoshop／PICT format

◎Operating environment

A Macintosh computer is required to handle this sample data disk. Although the data can be displayed on any Macintosh model, the data was created originally as 256 colors. The Macintosh monitor displays accurate hues that cannot be found in this book.

◎Getting started

Start your graphics software program, and click the Open command in the File pull-down menu to select the file you want.

These files have been created carefully and checked for viruses. Graphic-sha Publishing Co., Ltd. will not be responsible for any damage caused by files on this disk.

あとがき

いままで「コンピュータを使ったイラストレーションの技法」として位置づけた、入門のための本がありませんでした。この本の役割は、ここにあります。非常に簡単な方法のみで、多様な表現が可能なのだということを、例をあげて具体的に解説したつもりです。できればこの本を通して、それぞれの感性にあった表現と方法を開発、発見してほしいと願っています。ぼくの場合、一本の線に対する興味から、テクノロジーの発達と表現を考えるところまできてしまいました。そして、デジタルとアナログの境界を見ることになりました。それに対する飽きることのない思いは、今もなお続いています。たかが一本の線といえども人間にとって、はかりしれない奥行きがあるように思われます。原始時代の人間が引いた線から現代のコンピュータの引いた線までを見てみると、これからの「視覚表現における美の可能性」をよりいっそう追求することになりました。それをぼくは、「人間のもう一つの言葉」と呼んでいます。

この本を制作する上で、ぼくに多大な協力をしてくれたアシスタントの大野昌代さんと、共作のページに作品を提供していただいた若尾真一郎氏、そして英文翻訳をしてくれたスコット・ブラウス氏にお礼を述べるとともに、この新しいスタイルの技法書に対して深い理解を持って出版を勧め、実行してくれたグラフィック社の大田悟氏に心より感謝いたします。

『一つ目フクロウ』ステコン技法
" One-eyed owl" Stacom method

秋山孝
目白の仕事場にて

Postscript

Until now there have been no books for novices on the techniques of computer illustration. I intended to give examples with extremely simple techniques which made a wide range of expressions possible and then to explain them in detail. My hope is that through this book you will be able to develop and discover these expressions and techniques and the emotions from which they came. As far as my thoughts on the development and expression of technology are concerned, it is my fascination with a single line that has brought me this far. I can now see the border of the digital and analog worlds. This is a subject of which I never grow tired. I have been able to more deeply consider the aesthetic possibilities of visual sensation through my observation of lines, from the earliest lines drawn by primitive man, right up to the lines being drawn by computers today. I like to call these possibilities for visual sensation, "a secondary language of man."

I would like to thank my assistant, Masayo Ono, for the great amount of cooperation I received in the production of this book,Shinichiro Wakao for the contribution of his works to this book, and Scott Brause, for the English translation. I would also like to thank Satoru Ota of Graphic-sha Publishing Co., Ltd. whose deep understanding of this new type of instruction manual made its publication possible.

Takashi Akiyama
at Mejiro office

◎資料提供／アップルコンピュータ株式会社

1.MacintoshはApple Computer社の登録商標です。
2.Adobe Photoshopは米国アドビシステムズ社の米国内での登録商標です。
3.Adobe Illustratorは米国アドビシステムズ社の米国内での登録商標です。
4.その他、本書記載の商品名·名称等は各社の商標および登録商標です。なお、TM、Rマークは明記しておりません。

本書の内容に関する運用結果については責任を負いかねますので、ご了承ください。

秋山孝のMacイラスト講座
Getting Started as a Mac Illustrator

発　行 1994年 2月25日初版第1刷発行

著　者／秋山 孝　©Takashi Akiyama
装　丁／秋山 孝　©Takashi Akiyama
本文デザイン／秋山 孝事務所　©Takashi Akiyama
企画担当／大田 悟　Satoru Ota
翻　訳／スコット·ブラウス　Scott Brause

発行者／久世利郎
発行所／株式会社グラフィック社
〒102 東京都千代田区九段北1-9-12
Tel.03-3263-4318　Fax.03-5275-3579
印刷·製本／錦明印刷株式会社
乱丁·落丁はお取り替え致します。
著者に無断で複製及び使用を禁じます。

ISBN4-7661-0769-1 C3071